BOOK A
READING FOR CONCEPTS

"We learn to read in order to read to learn."

BOOK A
READING

FOR CONCEPTS

Third Edition

Phoenix Learning Resources
New York

Reading for Concepts
Third Edition
Book A
Contributing Authors for the Reading for Concepts Series

Linda Barton, feature writer for St. Louis Today
Roberta H. Berry, elementary school teacher, writer
Barbara Broeking, journalist and educational publications editor
Eth Clifford, author of many volumes of fiction and poetry for youth
Ellen Dolan, juvenile book author
Shirley Frederick, juvenile book author
Barbara R. Frey, Professor of Education, State University College, Buffalo, N.Y.
Ruth Harley, author and editor of young people's periodicals
Phyllis W. Kirk, children's book editor
Richard Kirk, author of science, social studies, and reading books for youth
Thomas D. Mantel, attorney and juvenile author
Marilyn F. Peachin, journalist and editor
James N. Rogers, author-editor of science and social studies resource books
James J. Pflaum, author and editor of current events periodicals
Gloria S. Rosenzweig, writer of children's books
Jean Shirley, author of juvenile books
Rosemary Winebrenner, editor of children's books
Jean White, journalist and writer of young people's reference materials

Vocabulary
Cynthia Merman, Reading and Language Specialist

Project Management and Production
Kane Publishing Services, Inc.

Cover Design
Pencil Point Studios

Text Design
Jim Darby

"I'm a Lucky Dog" on page 124 printed with permission of The Guidedog Foundation for the Blind, Smithtown, New York

Illustrators
James Cummings; Irene Semchyshyn; Portia Takajian, GAI

Cover Photography
Johnny Sundby/Dakota Skies Photography

ISBN 0–7915–2103–6

2 3 4 5 6 7 8 9 0 05 04 03 02 01

TABLE OF CONTENTS

TO THE TEACHER

Purpose

This book is one of eight in the series "Reading for Concepts." It was designed to provide an opportunity for young readers to grow in reading experience while exploring a wide variety of ideas contained in the major academic disciplines.

Two basic underlying concepts are reflected in this book. They are: *Change is a part of life*, and *Some changes happen faster than others*. The overriding concept in this book is the fact of change as a part of our lives. To illustrate these concepts, stories have been written around intriguing pieces of information that reflect these ideas. Content has been drawn from disciplines of history, biology, economics, Earth science, anthropology, mathematics, and geography. In this way, a wide array of content for meeting various interests has been assured.

A narrative follows stories 18, 36, and 54. The narratives, largely drawn from folk literature, will provide a change of pace and are "just for fun" types of stories.

Teaching Procedure

Detailed suggestions for presenting the selections in this book will be found on pages 15 and 16 in the Teacher's Guide. Difficult words, with grade-level definitions, are listed by story on pages 6-12. Important content-area proper nouns not defined in the text are included in this listing.

Following each article is a test, which is especially designed to improve specific skills in reading. The test items were created to incorporate the thinking skills reflected in Benjamin S. Bloom's *Taxonomy of Educational Objectives*, which is explained on pages 6-7 in the Teacher's Guide.

Concept Recapitulations

After students have completed each of the two sections of this book, you may conduct a discussion to tie together the information carried in the individual articles in terms of the overall concept. Guiding questions are found on page 13 for Concept I, and on page 93 for Concept II.

Have a few priming possibilities ready to suggest, or shape them out of earlier offerings from the group. Sophisticated statements and a review of specifics are not to be expected. Look for signs of mental play and the movement of information from one setting to another. It is perfectly reasonable to conclude with unanswered questions for students to ponder in retrospect. However, it is important to give students the satisfaction of enthusiastic acceptance of their early attempts at this type of open-ended speculation.

A. Turn to page 14. Look at the picture. Read the title. Think about what the story will say.

B. Study the words for this page on the list on page 6.

C. Read the story carefully.

D. Put your name and the title of the story on a sheet of paper.

Number from one to seven. Begin the test on the page next to the story.

1. This question asks you to remember something the story has told you. Which of the four choices will make the sentence say what the story says? Choose that statement.

2. This question asks you to find the word in the story that means the same as the words in slanting type.

3. This question asks you to find a word that is pointed out by a smaller word. Words like *he, they,* and *it* stand for words that have been written before. Read Question 3. Who was playing cards? The Earl. You can see that the word *He* means the *Earl.* There are clues to the right answer. Think about your answer.

4. This question wants you to think about the story. The answer is not in your book. Read the choices. Choose the sentence that is the very best guess you might make from the ideas you have read in the story.

5. This question requires much care. You must match the test sentence *word for word* with the one in the story. Does your choice begin like the one in the story? Are all the words in the same place?

6. This question asks you to choose a statement about the entire story. Don't select an idea that fits only one small part. Your answer should fit all of the story.

7. The question points out the place in your story where you will find the right word. You must find a word that is the opposite of the one in Question 7. Think about the meaning. For the first story, count the sentences from one to five in the first paragraph. Read the fifth sentence again. Write the word that is the opposite of *go.*

E. Check your work. The answers for the first test are given below. Your teacher may let you use the answer key for other tests.

F. Put the number correct at the top of your paper. Now go back and recheck the answers that were wrong. Do you see now how the correct answer was better?

G. Turn to page 170. The directions tell you how to put your score onto a record chart. Your teacher will tell you if you may write in the book. If not, he or she will help you make a copy for your notebook.

Looking for the Big Idea

See page 13 for big ideas to think about as you read.

Just for Fun

Your book has three longer stories that are just for fun. These stories, beginning on pages 50, 90, and 130, are from old folktales. There are no questions to answer.

Answers for Practice Test, page 15			
1. c	2. sandwich	3. Earl	4. c
5. a	6. c	7. stop	

Vocabulary Words and Definitions

PAGE 14

cards a game that uses pieces of paper with numbers and pictures

Earl in England, an important person

sandwich two pieces of bread with meat, cheese, or vegetables inside

wonderful very good

PAGE 16

masks pictures of people or animals worn over the face

medicine men healers or doctors

totem poles tall pieces of wood with pictures of people and animals carved in them

PAGE 18

collectors people who pick up things that are thrown away

scientists people who study the way we live

tools what people use to do a job

trash things that are thrown away

treasures very beautiful or rare things

PAGE 20

cables strong wires that hold something up

kites pieces of cloth or paper with a long string, moved by the wind

lightning a flash of light in a rainstorm

wire a long, thin, round piece of metal

PAGE 22

beaver a furry animal that lives in the water and on land

dams piles of dirt and rocks that go across a river and slow the water

streams small rivers

trapped caught

PAGE 24

calculators machines that do arithmetic

facts things that are true

grapes small, sweet fruit

PAGE 26

acorn a small seed from an oak tree; if you plant an acorn, an oak tree will grow

dug took from the ground

shoot a small part of a plant

squirrel a small animal with a long, furry tail

PAGE 28

ancestor a parent or grandparent; a person or animal that lived long ago

hunters people who kill animals for food

jobs work; things we are supposed to do

Stone Age a time millions of years ago when people learned to make tools out of stone

tame friendly, well behaved

wolf a wild animal related to the dog

PAGE 30

forest a place with a lot of trees where many animals live

hoof a horse's foot

millions very many; more than 1,000,000

running moving very quickly

PAGE 32

hummingbird a very small bird with a long beak that makes a noise like a hum

liquid something that is wet, like water or juice

nectar something sweet that flowers and plants make; birds and insects eat nectar

peas small, round, green vegetables

PAGE 34

giant very, very big

rot fall apart

PAGE 36

pads small, soft spots

snore a loud noise some people make when they sleep

sticky like glue or paste

whistles makes a high noise through the mouth

PAGE 38

farmed grew vegetables

useful helpful; solves a problem

PAGE 40

machine something that does work for people

marbles small, round pieces of glass

threads long, thin pieces of cloth

PAGE 42

families the people you live with; fathers, mothers, children

skills things we know how to do

Swiss people who live in or come from Switzerland

Switzerland a country in Europe

Tibet a small country in Asia, near India

Tibetans people who live in or come from Tibet

PAGE 44

ads pictures and words describing something to buy

advertising talking about or showing pictures of things so that people will want to buy them

later at some time in the future

newspapers pages that tell what is happening in the world; newspapers have ads

printing making letters and words with a machine, instead of writing by hand

PAGE 46

cannot is not able to do something

cereal a breakfast food made of corn, rice, or wheat, usually eaten with milk

vote to choose the person you like best

PAGE 48

adobe bricks made of mud that are dried in the sun

clay a material that is soft like mud and can be made into many shapes; clay hardens in the sun or in an oven

dirt earth or ground

mesa a high, flat piece of ground

pueblo a group of houses that some Native Americans live in

PAGES 50–53

redbud a kind of tree with red and pink flowers

PAGE 54

airplanes machines that fly and carry people from place to place

breathe to take in air through the nose

dizzy silly or mixed up

heart a part of the body that keeps us alive by moving the blood

lungs parts of the body that help us breathe

PAGE 56

fossil parts of a plant or animal that died many years ago

leaf a green part of a plant or tree that grows from the stem

PAGE 58

mountaintops the tops of very high hills

seashells the hard, outside parts of some animals that live in the ocean

PAGE 60

Canada a large country north of the United States

glacier a very, very big piece of ice that moves slowly over land

melt to change from ice to water

PAGE 62

Colorado a state in the midwestern United States

dug cut a hole in

Grand Canyon a giant hole in the ground in Arizona, a state in the midwestern United States

layers flat pieces laid one on top of the other

mules animals that people can ride; they look like small horses

PAGE 64

cone a tall, round shape that is bigger at the bottom than at the top

lava hot, melted rock, that comes out of a volcano

Mexico a country in Central America, south of the United States

volcano a mountain with a hole in the top that lava comes out of

PAGE 66

factories buildings where people work to make things

villages small groups of houses where people live together

PAGE 68

aren't are not

coughing trying to get something out of the throat

dishcloth a cloth used to dry dishes

pepper a black-colored spice used in food

PAGE 68 continued

string a long, thin piece of material used to tie things together or to pull something

warts hard bumps on the skin

PAGE 70

language the words people use to talk to each other

pupils students in school

Romans people who live in or come from Rome, a city in Italy

Rome the capital of Italy, a country in Europe

PAGE 72

cinnamon a spice used to make desserts taste good

spices things added to food to make it taste better

PAGE 74

armies groups of people who fight against other people

drum a musical instrument that you hit with a stick

message words sent from one person to another

pigeons birds that remember where they live and can find their way home

runner someone who runs from one place to another to give people messages

PAGE 76

benches seats that two or three people can sit on together

berries small fruits

dunce someone who is not smart

ink liquid used in a pen for writing

odd strange or unusual

PAGE 76 continued

pioneer the first person to do something or go some place

slates pieces of stone you can write on with chalk

PAGE 78

California a state in the west part of the United States, on the Pacific Ocean

cloth material clothes are made of

gold a yellow-colored metal that is worth a lot of money

mine to dig underground for gold

miner someone who digs for gold

wagon a wooden truck without a roof, usually pulled by horses

PAGE 80

exactly just right

knot a lump in a piece of string

numerals numbers, such as 1, 2, 3

PAGE 82

Egypt a country in the north of Africa

rule to be in charge of a country, like a king or a president

ruler someone who rules or is in charge of a country

PAGE 84

calendar a list of the days and dates of the weeks and months of a year

PAGE 86

dots very small colored-in circles

Egyptians people who live in or come from Egypt, a country in Africa

Mayans native people who live in Central and South America

South America the continent to the south of the United States

PAGE 88

ancient very old; from a long time ago

subtract to take away from; to make smaller

PAGES 90–92

bushy having lots of fur or hair

hop jump up and down

stretch to get longer

PAGE 94

elk large deer with horns

soil dirt that plants grow in

Yellowstone Park a big area in western United States, that has forests, mountains, and wild animals

PAGE 96

built made or constructed

butterflies beautiful insects whose wings are different colors

Illinois a state in central United States

insects small animals with eight legs; bugs

sprays liquids that come out of small holes in a bottle, like rain or a shower

PAGE 98

museum a building in which things are kept; for instance, an art museum has pictures in it

PAGE 100

chess a game played on a board; you win if your 16 pieces capture the other player's 16 pieces

prices how much money things cost

spaceship a kind of airplane that flies in outer space

spell to write a word correctly

write to put letters and words on paper

PAGE 102
desert a place that is hot and dry and gets very little rain

gas a liquid used to drive cars or heat homes

nomads people who move from one place to another; people who don't live in one place

pipeline a long, hollow piece of metal that takes gas and oil from one place to another

tribe a group of people

PAGE 104
licorice the root of a plant that is made into black-colored candy

majesty a king or queen

PAGE 106
bumblebee a yellow insect with black stripes that makes a sound like "bzzz"

clover a short, green plant that cows and other animals like to eat

pollen a dust made by plants; bees and other insects carry pollen from one plant to another, which makes more plants grow

PAGE 108
den an underground home for an animal

lizard an animal without fur that can live in water or on land

stems the parts of plants that grow out of the ground and hold up the flowers and leaves

store to hold or save

PAGE 110
dinosaurs very big lizards that lived millions of years ago

dragonfly an insect with big wings

PAGE 112
Africa the continent south of Europe

apes big monkeys; gorillas

PAGE 112 continued
bananas yellow fruit that is a favorite of chimpanzees

chimpanzees small monkeys that like to play

jungle a hot place with lots of trees and animals

shy afraid of people

trust to believe in

wild not tame; not used to being with people

PAGE 114
buttercups small yellow flowers

daffodils yellow or orange spring flowers

plain simple; small

search to look for

PAGE 116
carefully slowly; paying attention

empty with nothing inside

locust an insect; a grasshopper

tight too small

PAGE 118
electricity makes lightbulbs and machines work

fertile able to grow plants

flood to cover with water, from heavy rains

Mississippi River the second-longest river in the United States

PAGE 120
style the way something looks

wigs fake hair worn on the head

PAGE 122
bars rectangle shapes, for instance, candy bars

English people who live in England, an island country in Europe

metal gold or silver

Spanish people who live in Spain, a country in southern Europe

PAGE 122 continued
special different
worth how much money something costs

PAGE 124
behave to act correctly; do what you are told
blind cannot see
gentle quiet; tame
guide dog a dog that has learned to take its owner from one place to another
leash something used to hold a dog so it doesn't run away

PAGE 126
Indian a Native American; person who lived in America before Columbus arrived
leaders the people in charge who make the rules
moccasins soft leather shoes, usually made by Native Americans

PAGE 128
dyes liquids that change the color of something
fibers long strings from plants, used to make cloth
flax a kind of plant whose fibers can be made into cloth
wove used a machine to make fibers into cloth

PAGES 130–133
shade a place that is dark and cool because there is no sun; shadow
stupid not smart
understand know why something happens

PAGE 134
Great Lakes five big lakes in the United States near Canada: Huron, Ontario, Michigan, Erie, and Superior

PAGE 136
herds large groups of animals
PAGE 136 continued
Lapland a large, very cold part of northern Europe
reindeer large deer that live in very cold areas

PAGE 138
current moving water
Indian Ocean one of the five oceans of Earth, south of India and east of Africa
monsoon very strong winds and rains

PAGE 140
farther a longer way; a greater distance
shore the land near the ocean
shoreline where the land and ocean meet
toward in the direction of
West Indian from the West Indies, islands in the Caribbean Sea

PAGE 142
castles big stone houses that kings and queens lived in
chimneys parts of houses on the roof; smoke from a fireplace goes up the chimney
strange odd; unusual; funny looking

PAGE 144
battle a fight, usually between two armies
construction workers people who build things, such as office buildings
helmets hats worn so the head doesn't get hurt
plastic a hard, light material
spears long sticks with a sharp point at one end

PAGE 146
ghost the spirit of a dead person

PAGE 148

gatekeeper a person who guards the door or entrance to a place

pike a long spear

stuck cannot move

turnpikes roads that charge people money to use

PAGE 150

basketball a ball game played by two teams; the team that throws more balls into a basket wins

net a basket made of string

peach a sweet, round fruit

PAGE 152

blubber a whale's fat

oil liquid from melting a whale's blubber

polish something that makes things shiny

whales very big animals that live in the ocean

PAGE 154

buffalo big animals like cows; their meat is used for food

explorers people who go to a new place to learn about it

quickly fast

Sioux a Native American tribe

Spain a country in Europe

PAGE 156

chains metal rings that hold something in place

libraries places where books are kept

Page 158

rods measures that equal 16 1/2 feet

rood a length that equals 16 feet

PAGE 160

fist a person's hand when the fingers and thumb are closed

grandparents the parents of your parents

heel the back of the foot

sock a piece of clothing worn on the foot

PAGE 162

later afterward

numerals numbers

zero none; 0

PAGE 164

buildings places with walls and a roof, such as schools, churches, stores, and houses

cracks opens up and leaves a hole

earthquake shaking of the Earth, which causes damage

fifteen the number 15; one more than 14

hospitals places that help people who are sick or hurt

pipes metal tubes that carry water

San Francisco a city in northern California

PAGE 166

angle the place where two lines meet

stretchers people who pull something tight

tight not loose

PAGE 168

abacus a tool for counting and adding; it uses rows of beads that stand for numbers

Asia a large continent that contains Russia, China, and India

beads small ball-shaped objects

counters things used to count how many

pebbles small stones or rocks

I
Change Is a Part of Life

In this section, you will read about many things that change. You will read about these things in the areas of anthropology (the study of people), biology (the science that studies how things grow), Earth science, geography (the study of the features of Earth), history (study of the past), economics (the study of the making of goods to use), and mathematics.

Keep these questions in mind when you are reading.
1. How many ways can I see that changes took place?
2. Did people want to change?
3. Have all the changes affected me?
4. Were the changes usually good?
5. Does everything change in the long run?

Look on pages 6-9 for help with words you don't understand in this section.

The Earl Was Busy

1   The Earl of Sandwich was busy. He was playing cards. He liked games. He played all day. He did not stop to eat. He played all night. He did not sleep.

2   At last the Earl was hungry. He did not want to take time for dinner.

3   "Bring me my meat," he said. "Put it between two pieces of bread."

4   The Earl ate his bread and meat. The meat did not get on his fingers. He kept on playing cards.

5   "That looks good," his friends thought. They put their meat between two pieces of bread, too. They liked the way it tasted. "What a wonderful way to eat," they said.

6   Other people liked this new way of eating, too. They wanted their bread and meat fixed the way the Earl of Sandwich had his. What did they ask for?

1. The Earl asked for
   - a. eggs and milk.
   - b. cake.
   - c. meat between bread.
   - d. apples

2. The word in the story that means *meat between slices of bread* is _____.

3. The story says, "The Earl of Sandwich was busy. *He* was playing cards." The word *he* means the _____.

4. Which of the following does this story lead you to believe?
   - a. The Earl of Sandwich had no friends.
   - b. The Earl of Sandwich was not a very smart man.
   - c. The sandwich was named for an Earl of Sandwich.

5. Why could the Earl go on playing cards? (Which sentence is exactly like the one in your book?)
   - a. The meat did not get on his fingers.
   - b. The meat was all gone.
   - c. The meat on his fingers helped him win.

6. The main idea of the whole story is
   - a. that most people sleep all day.
   - b. that the Earl never got hungry.
   - c. why the first sandwich was made.

7. The opposite of *go* (in sentence five) is _____.

Do You Ever Wear A Mask?

1   People have been using masks for thousands of years. Masks have been used in many ways. Some tribes wore masks when they went to war. They thought the masks helped them win. Others thought that wearing animal masks would make them strong. Others thought the world was run by gods. They made masks for these gods. The people danced before the masks. The people hoped the dancing would keep the gods happy.

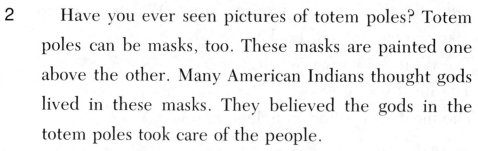

2   Have you ever seen pictures of totem poles? Totem poles can be masks, too. These masks are painted one above the other. Many American Indians thought gods lived in these masks. They believed the gods in the totem poles took care of the people.

3   Indian medicine men and medicine women had masks. With the masks on, these Indians thought they could make sick people well.

4   Today, doctors wear masks. What other people wear masks? Do you ever wear a mask?

1. Animal masks were supposed to make people
   - a. beautiful.
   - b. strong.
   - c. kind.
   - d. happy.

2. The word in the story that means *coverings that hide faces* is _____.

3. The story says, "Some tribes wore masks when *they* went to war." The word *they* means _____.

4. Which of the following does this story lead you to believe?
   - a. We use masks in different ways today.
   - b. You have to wear a mask when you take medicine.
   - c. You can never wear a mask.

5. What do we know about totem poles? (Which sentence is exactly like the one in your book?)
   - a. Totem poles are trees that fall down.
   - b. Totem poles can be masks, too.
   - c. Totem poles are poles on ships.

6. The main idea of the whole story is that
   - a. masks have been used in many ways.
   - b. totem poles make people sick.
   - c. Indians do not like medicine.

7. The opposite of *lose* (in sentence four) is _____.

Trash or Treasures

1   Trash collectors come down the street. They take away cans and papers. They take away broken toys. They take all the things we do not want.

2   Thousands of years ago, people had trash, too. They threw away old baskets and broken bowls. They threw away broken tools. Time went by. The trash was covered up.

3   Today, scientists dig to find these things. They look at the broken bowls and baskets. They look at the tools. They learn many things about the people of long ago.

4   Some of the old things are beautiful. We do not call them trash. We call them treasures. We save them and take care of them.

5   A thousand years from now, people may find our trash. They may see old cans and papers. They may find such things as broken clocks and old toys. Do you think our trash will become their treasure?

1. Long ago, people threw away
    a. old baskets.   c. books.
    b. dolls.   d. candy.

2. The word in the story that means *old, broken things no one wants*

    is _____.

3. The story says, "Trash collectors come down the street.
    They take away cans and papers." The word *they* means

    _____.

4. Which of the following does the story lead you to believe?
    a. Scientists want to know about people of long ago.
    b. All scientists wear white coats when they are working.
    c. The trash collector is a scientist.

5. Why do scientists look at the things they find? (Which sentence
    is exactly like the one in your book?)
    a. They learn how to throw many old things away.
    b. They learn how to look at tools no one wants.
    c. They learn many things about the people of long ago.

6. The main idea of the whole story is that
    a. baskets are good for holding trash.
    b. trash collectors take away all our good things.
    c. some things of long ago are treasures today.

7. The opposite of *new* (paragraph two, sentence two) is _____.

A Sky Full of Fish

1   The sky is full of fish and animals. The fish and animals are kites. It is Kite Day in the park.

2   Kites go far back in time. Once people believed kites could carry their thoughts to the gods. Many people flew kites over their houses at night. They thought this kept them safe from all bad things at night.

3   Kites are fun. But they also have been of great help to us. People have used kites to learn more about the weather. Kites have been used in building bridges. Heavy wire cables for bridges have been pulled across water with the use of kites.

4   Once a great American put a key on a kite. He wanted to know more about lightning. Do you know who he was?

1. Kites flying over the houses at night were to keep people
   - a. happy.
   - c. quiet.
   - b. safe.
   - d. at home.

2. The word in the story that means *heavy wires across bridges* is _____.

3. The story says, "Kites are fun. But *they* have also been of great help to us." The word *they* means _____.

4. Which of the following does this story lead you to believe?
   - a. Today we fly kites for fun.
   - b. Today we fly kites to keep bad things away.
   - c. Today we use kites to hold our keys.

5. How have kites been used? (Which sentence is exactly like the one in your book?)
   - a. People have used kites to learn more about outer space.
   - b. People have used kites to learn more about the weather.
   - c. People have used kites to learn more about how to fly.

6. The main idea of the whole story is that
   - a. kites have been used in many ways.
   - b. it is hard to build a bridge.
   - c. fish like to fly kites.

7. The opposite of *under* (paragraph two, sentence three) is _____.

Busy as a Beaver

1   Beavers like water. They live near streams. Beavers work to make dams. They make them out of rocks, mud, and sticks. The dam goes across the stream. It stops the water and makes a pond. The beavers make houses in the pond. The water in the pond is cold. Beavers have beautiful thick fur to keep them warm.

2   Years ago many people trapped the beavers. They used the beaver fur to make hats and coats. Soon the beavers were almost gone. The dams were gone. The ponds were gone. The fish and the frogs in the ponds were gone. The birds that eat the fish and frogs were gone. The land changed.

3   People said, "Beavers are good for the land. They make homes for fish and frogs, birds and bugs." They stopped trapping the beavers. The beavers came back. The dams came back. The ponds came back. Now the beavers are busy again.

1. Beavers make

     a. traps.   b.   hats.   c.   dams.   d. coats.

2. The word in the story that means *something that holds water back*

   is _____.

3. The story says, "Beavers make dams. *They* make them out of rocks, mud, and sticks." The word *they* means _____.

4. Which of the following does this story lead you to believe?

     a. The beavers' work helps other animals.

     b. Beavers don't like cold water.

     c. Beavers like to play.

5. How did people use beaver fur? (Which sentence is exactly like the one in your book?)

     a. Beaver fur was used to make dams.

     b. They used the beaver fur for houses.

     c. They used the beaver fur to make hats and coats.

6. The main idea of the whole story is

     a. beavers have thick fur.

     b. the beavers went away and never came back.

     c. beavers change the land where they live.

7. The opposite of *hot* (paragraph one, sentence eight) is

   _____.

Old and New Ways to Add

1   Do you like grapes? Pretend that you ate five grapes. Then you ate five more. How many did you eat? Put a mark on a paper for each grape, like this: ⦀⦀ ⦀⦀. Count the marks by fives. You ate 10 grapes. This is an old way of adding.

2   Now pretend that you eat a whole stem of grapes and make a mark for each grape. Then you count the marks. It takes a long time. This way of adding is very slow.

3   There is a faster way to add. You can learn the number facts. You already know that 2 + 3 = 5, and that 5 + 5 = 10. You can add big numbers quickly if you know the facts.

4   Today we have machines like calculators and computers to help us add numbers. Stores use computers to add up what you buy. A calculator can fit in your pocket.

5   Machines have made adding numbers quick and easy. They have changed the way we do math. But we still must learn the number facts!

1. A machine that adds fast is a

   a. stem.   b. mark.   c. fact.   d. computer.

2. The word in the story that means *small round fruit* is

   _____.

3. The story says, "Machines have made adding numbers quick and easy. *They* have changed the way we do math." The word *they* means _____.

4. Which of the following does the story lead you to believe?

   a. Stores use computers because they add numbers quickly.

   b. Stores use computers because they are small.

   c. Stores don't use computers.

5. What can you do if you know number facts? (Which sentence is exactly like the one in your book?)

   a. You can eat lots of grapes.

   b. You can use a calculator.

   c. You can add big numbers quickly if you know the facts.

6. The main idea of the whole story is

   a. it is easy to count by fives.

   b. machines have changed the way we add.

   c. 2 + 3 = 5.

7. The opposite of *fast* (paragraph two, sentence four) is

   _____.

The Squirrel and the Acorn

1   An acorn is a seed. It holds food for a new plant. It holds life for a new plant. Oak trees grow from acorns.

2   In the fall, a squirrel ran across a yard. It ran to a big oak tree. It looked for acorns. When the squirrel found them, it hid the acorns in the ground.

3   In the winter, it dug up the acorns to eat. When spring came, one acorn was still in the ground. The spring rains made the acorn soft. The sun made the ground warm. The acorn began to grow. A root went down. A small white shoot pushed up.

4   The small white shoot pushed through the top of the ground. Two small leaves came out. They were oak leaves.

5   Another oak tree was growing. It would become a big tree some day. Its acorns would drop to the ground. Would another squirrel find them and plant another tree?

1. The squirrel dug up the acorns in
    a. spring.   c. summer.
    b. fall.   d. winter.

2. The word in the story that means *a plant beginning to push out of the ground* is _____ .

3. The story says, "Another oak tree was growing. *It* would become a big tree some day." The word *it* means _____ .

4. Which of the following does this story lead you to believe?
    a. Animals can spread seeds.
    b. Animals stop trees from growing.
    c. Many squirrels don't like acorns.

5. What happened to the acorn that was left in the ground? (Which sentence is exactly like the one in your book?)
    a. The acorn looked for the squirrel.
    b. The acorn began to die.
    c. The acorn began to grow.

6. The main idea of the whole story is that
    a. an oak tree grew from an acorn a squirrel planted.
    b. squirrels like to live and play in big trees.
    c. an oak tree cannot grow from an acorn.

7. The opposite of *hard* (paragraph three, sentence three) is

    _____ .

Pet from the Stone Age

1   Dogs are our friends. They work for us. They hunt with us. They play with us. But once, all over the world, dogs were wild.

2   Dogs go back to the Stone Age. All dogs had the same ancestor. It is believed that this ancestor was much like a wolf. Other animals, like the fox, came from this ancestor, too.

3   Thousands of years ago, people began to tame the wild dogs. When the dogs were tame, they were trained. The strong dogs became working animals. They were trained to pull heavy loads. They learned to keep watch over sheep and other animals. Working dogs had other jobs, too.

4   Some dogs were not strong. But they could help hunters find game. Other dogs were best as pets.

5   At first, there were only a few kinds of dogs. Today, there are more than 400 kinds.

1. We believe the ancestor of the dog was much like the
   a. fox.   c. wolf.
   b. cow.   d. fish.

2. The word in the story that means *an animal far back in another animal's family* is _____.

3. The story says, "When the dogs were tame, *they* were trained." The word *they* means _____.

4. Which of the following does this story lead you to believe?
   a. Animals never change.
   b. Most cats are just like dogs.
   c. People have helped change animals.

5. What happened to some strong dogs? (Which sentence is exactly like the one in your book?)
   a. The strong dogs turned into foxes.
   b. The strong dogs became working animals.
   c. The strong dogs did not like to work hard.

6. The main idea of the whole story is that
   a. dogs and people have been friends for a long time.
   b. foxes are better than dogs for pulling heavy loads.
   c. all animals cannot be pets.

7. The opposite of *weak* (paragraph four, sentence one) is _____.

A Horse No Bigger Than a Cat

1   Have you ever seen a horse with toes? Millions of years ago, horses had many toes. They had four toes on each front foot. They had three toes on each back foot. The horses were no bigger than cats.

2   These small horses lived in the forest. Their many toes helped the horses run over the soft, wet ground.

3   It was very hot in the forest. But the weather changed. It became cold. Many trees could not live in cold weather. The trees died and fell. Open fields took the place of forests. The sun made the ground dry and hard.

4   Horses began to change, too. They began to get bigger. This took a long time. On the dry, hard land, horses needed only their middle toes for running. Their middle toes became hard. After a long while, horses had only one hard toe on each foot. We call this hard toe a hoof.

1. Long ago, the horse had four toes on each of its
    a. front feet.   c. back feet.
    b. left feet.   d. right feet.

2. The word in the story that means *many trees together* is

    _____.

3. The story says, "But the weather changed. *It* became cold."

    The word *it* means _____.

4. Which of the following does this story lead you to believe?
    a. Animals have always been the same as they are today.
    b. When the earth changed, animals began to change, too.
    c. Weather stays the same all year long around the world.

5. What did the horses need on dry, hard land? (Which sentence is exactly like the one in your book?)
    a. On the dry, hard land, horses needed only their middle toes for running.
    b. On the dry, hard land, the horses needed a lot of room for running.
    c. On the dry, hard land, horses needed to get smaller.

6. The main idea of the whole story is that
    a. the weather never changes.
    b. cats were once much bigger than horses.
    c. horses changed very much over the years.

7. The opposite of *dry* (in sentence seven) is _____.

The Smallest Bird

1   The little bird took nectar from a flower. This sweet liquid was food for the bird. It used its long bill to get at the nectar deep in the flower. The little bird was a hummingbird. Hummingbirds are the smallest birds in the world.

2   The hummingbird made a nest. The nest looked like a very small cup. Soon there were two white eggs in the nest. The eggs were no bigger than peas. Little birds came out of the eggs. They were very hungry. The parent birds brought them nectar. They put their long bills down the necks of the babies to feed them nectar.

3   The baby birds stayed in the nest almost three weeks. They left the nest when they were big enough and strong enough to fly. Soon they could build their own nests. They could get their own nectar. They could feed their own very small babies.

1. The hummingbird got nectar from a
   - a. nest.
   - b. flower.
   - c. bird.
   - d. cup.

2. The word in the story that means *the smallest bird in the world*

   is _____.

3. The story says, "Little birds came out of the eggs. *They* were very

   hungry." The word *they* means _____.

4. Which of the following does this story lead you to believe?
   - a. Hummingbirds have to eat only green peas to stay alive.
   - b. Hummingbirds need the nectar from flowers to stay alive.
   - c. Hummingbirds don't know how to make nests.

5. How big were the hummingbird's eggs? (Which sentence is exactly like the one in your book?)
   - a. The eggs were no bigger than peas.
   - b. The eggs were no bigger than cups.
   - c. The eggs were no bigger than marbles.

6. The main idea of the whole story is that
   - a. hummingbirds are big birds.
   - b. birds' nests are made out of tiny green peas.
   - c. the mother bird takes care of the baby birds.

7. The opposite of *left* (paragraph three, sentence one) is

   _____.

Room to Grow

1   Lightning hit a giant tree in the forest. The tree died. It fell to the ground. Soon the tree began to rot.

2   Seeds from other trees fell to the ground. These seeds could not grow. There were too many plants on the forest floor. But one seed fell on the dead tree. It was high off the ground. This seed had room to grow.

3   A new plant grew from the seed that fell on the dead tree. The new plant put out new roots. The roots grew into the rotting tree. The roots went through the tree to the ground.

4   The dead tree rotted more and more. But the new plant grew. The rotting tree was its food. The new plant reached for the sun. It grew tall and strong. Soon there was another tree in the forest.

1. When a tree dies and falls to the ground it begins to
   a. rot.   c. bleed.
   b. grow.   d. bite.

2. The word in the story that means *the ground in the forest on which many plants grow* is _____.

3. The story says, "The tree died. *It* fell to the ground." The word *it* means _____.

4. Which of the following does this story lead you to believe?
   a. Seeds do not need room to grow.
   b. Some seeds plant themselves.
   c. Seeds make trees die.

5. Where did one seed fall? (Which sentence is exactly like the one in your book?)
   a. But one seed fell on the dead tree.
   b. But one seed fell on a new plant.
   c. But one seed was hit by lightning.

6. The main idea of the whole story is that
   a. a new plant can grow out of a dead plant.
   b. lightning cannot hit a tree.
   c. seeds do not need room to grow well.

7. The opposite of *low* (paragraph two, sentence five) is _____.

The Frog That Changes Color

1   Birds live in trees. Squirrels live in trees. But did you know that some frogs live in trees, too?

2   The tree frog is hard to find. This frog can change color. On green leaves, it stays green. On a brown branch, it turns brown. Some tree frogs can change from green to gold or blue.

3   Tree frogs have long legs and wide feet. They have sticky pads at the ends of their toes. These sticky toe pads keep the tree frogs from falling.

4   Tree frogs have different colors and markings on their skins. Their eyes are different, too. Some have green eyes, some gray. Some frogs' eyes are gold, and some are bright red.

5   The sounds they make in spring and summer are different, too. One frog makes a sound like a dog barking. Another frog makes a loud noise like a snore. There is even a frog that whistles!

1. Tree frogs have sticky pads on the ends of their
     a. noses.   c. arms.
     b. tails.   d. toes.

2. The word in the story that means *different signs on an animal's skin* is _____.

3. The story says, "This frog can change color. On green leaves, *it* stays green." The word *it* means _____.

4. Which of the following does this story lead you to believe?
     a. There are many different kinds of frogs.
     b. All frogs have red eyes and make the same sound.
     c. Frogs all look the same.

5. Why is the tree frog hard to find? (Which sentence is exactly like the one in your book?)
     a. This frog can stand on its toes.
     b. This frog can make a dog bark.
     c. This frog can change color.

6. The main idea of the whole story is that
     a. squirrels do not want frogs in their trees.
     b. the tree frog is a special kind of frog.
     c. dogs bark like frogs.

7. The opposite of *short* (paragraph three, sentence one) is

   _____.

Let's Trade

1   Let's trade! Will you take a piece of cake for an apple? A good book for a game? A toy boat for a car?

2   Long ago, people had to get what they wanted by trading. Some people farmed the land. Other people made tools. Tools were traded for food.

3   All kinds of trading took place. If people had too much meat, they could trade it for corn. They could trade animal skins for tools. Sometimes a person would trade a day's work for a place to sleep.

4   Many useful things were traded. But people wanted pretty things, too. A farmer might trade milk for a piece of beautiful cloth.

5   Even today we trade with one another. When you buy candy, do you pay for it with bear fat? Of course not! You use money. But you are still trading. You are still giving one thing for another.

1. A day's work was traded for
    a. a place to sleep.   c. games.
    b. an apple.   d. toy boats.

2. The word in the story that means *giving one thing for another* is _____.

3. The story says, "If people had too much meat, they could trade *it* for corn." The word *it* means _____.

4. Which of the following does this story lead you to believe?
    a. Long ago, people might trade a pig for a piece of silk.
    b. People long ago used to trade bear fat for animals.
    c. People long ago didn't know very much about trading.

5. How do you trade today? (Which sentence is exactly like the one in your book?)
    a. You use money.
    b. You use chickens.
    c. You trade when you hear a bell ring.

6. The main idea of the whole story is that
    a. people trade only for food and a place to sleep.
    b. people never traded any useful things long ago.
    c. people trade things for what they need and want.

7. The opposite of *yesterday* (paragraph five, sentence one) is _____.

A Thread 100 Miles Long

1   Would you wear leaves or grass? Would you wear an animal skin? No? Long ago, people had to wear what they could find. They had no cloth.

2   Would you wear coal or milk or grain? No, again? Are you sure?

3   Ways have been found to use these things for clothes. Milk or coal or grain may be put with other things and cooked. The heat turns these things into a liquid. The liquid runs out through little holes. Now, it becomes long threads. The threads are fine and strong. Cloth is made from the threads.

4   Today, cloth can even be made from glass. First the glass is shaped into marbles. These are made very hot in a machine. The machine has many little holes. The marbles are pushed through the holes. Glass from the marbles comes out in long threads. One glass marble can make a thread almost 100 miles long!

5   Can you name some things made from glass thread?

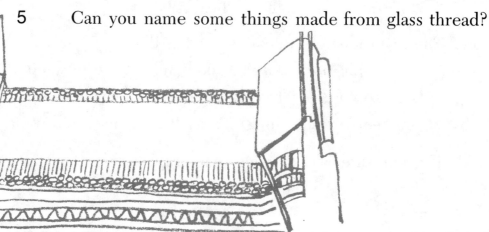

1. Cloth can be made from
   a. bananas.
   b. glass.
   c. holes.
   d. clay.

2. The word in the story that means *something that is not solid* is _____.

3. The story says "Long ago, people had to wear what *they* could find." The word *they* means _____.

4. Which of the following does this story lead you to believe?
   a. Glass thread can be made to make many things.
   b. Animals have to wear clothes made of grass.
   c. No one can make threads that are long.

5. What are the threads like? (Which sentence is exactly like the one in your book?)
   a. The threads are fine and strong.
   b. The threads are thin and long.
   c. The threads are much too long.

6. The main idea of the whole story is that
   a. people can only use milk and grain for food.
   b. different things have been used to make clothes.
   c. machines become 100 miles long when making cloth.

7. The opposite of *big* (paragraph three, sentence four) is _____.

A Land Almost Like Home

1   Tashi lives in Switzerland. But that is not where she was born. She is from Tibet, a country far from Switzerland. It is a beautiful country, high up in the mountains. The people are called Tibetans.

2   Tashi loved Tibet, but she had to leave. When she was young, some people took over her country. They did bad things and many people were killed. Tashi and her family left to find a better place to live. They went to Switzerland.

3   Life changed for the Tibetans in Switzerland. Some Tibetan children had no mother or father. Swiss families took care of them. The Swiss also helped the Tibetans to find work and learn new skills. The Tibetans learned to talk like the Swiss.

4   Today Tashi's family misses their country. But they like Switzerland. It has high mountains, as Tibet does. It is a good place to live.

5   At home, the Tibetans teach their children about Tibet. They cook Tibetan foods. They celebrate Tibetan holidays. There have been many changes in the lives of the Tibetans in Switzerland. But they have not forgotten their past.

1. Tibet is a

    a. town.   b. country.   c. mountain.   d. person.

2. The word in the story that means *the people of Tibet* is

    _____.

3. The story says, "Some Tibetan children had no mother or father. Swiss families took care of *them*." The word *them* means

    _____.

4. Which of the following does the story lead you to believe?

    a. The Tibetans like to live in the mountains.

    b. The Tibetans don't want to work.

    c. The Tibetans didn't like Tibet.

5. What did the Swiss do for the Tibetans? (Which sentence is exactly like the one in your book?)

    a. The Swiss also gave the Tibetans food.

    b. The Swiss also gave the Tibetans money.

    c. The Swiss also helped the Tibetans to find work and learn new skills.

6. The main idea of the whole story is

    a. the Tibetans in Switzerland are poor.

    b. Swiss life is not at all like Tibetan life.

    c. the Tibetans learned how to live in Switzerland.

7. The opposite of *low* (paragraph 1, sentence four) is _____.

Walking, Talking Ads

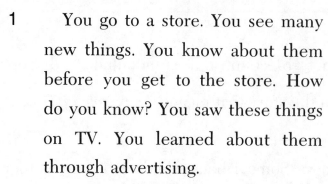

1   You go to a store. You see many new things. You know about them before you get to the store. How do you know? You saw these things on TV. You learned about them through advertising.

2   People have been advertising for thousands of years. Long ago, men called "criers" walked up and down the streets. They shouted about things that were being sold.

3   Later, people met at one place. This place was a market. Some people came to sell. Other people came to buy. But only those people who were at the market knew what was being sold.

4   When people learned about printing, things changed. Soon there were newspapers. Many people read the newspapers. They saw many ads in the papers. Later, more people saw and listened to the ads on TV. Are the people who sell to us "criers"?

1. When you go to a store you see
   a. singers.
   c. many new things.
   b. people crying.
   d. dancers.

2. The word in the story that means *papers printed every day that tell the news* is _____ .

3. The story says, "Many people read the newspapers. *They* saw many ads in the papers." The word *they* means _____ .

4. Which of the following does this story lead you to believe?
   a. We go to the store to read the newspaper.
   b. We go to the store to buy things we hear about.
   c. We go to the store to look at the ads on television.

5. How long have people been advertising? (Which sentence is exactly like the one in your book?)
   a. People have been advertising since yesterday.
   b. People have not been advertising very much at all.
   c. People have been advertising for thousands of years.

6. The main idea of the whole story is that
   a. people advertise to sell things.
   b. people cried when they had to advertise.
   c. people went to the market.

7. The opposite of *sell* (paragraph three, sentence four) is

   _____ .

Can You Vote?

1   You know that men and women vote. They vote for the people who run our country. But did you know that you vote, too? Did you know that your vote is very important?

2   You go to the store. Your parent picks up a box of cereal. You say, "No! Not that one!" You pick another cereal. You have just voted for one cereal. You have just voted against another cereal. If enough people vote against a cereal, it does not sell. Soon the company must stop making this cereal. Your vote makes this happen.

3   You see a new toy. You buy it. You don't like it. You tell your friends not to buy it. Soon the toy company cannot sell this toy. It makes a different toy that you will want to own.

4   You are very important. You are the one with the vote.

1. You vote against something by saying
        a. hello.   c. maybe.
        b. good-by.   d. no.

2. The word in the story that means *to choose one thing and not the other* is _____ .

3. The story says, "You see a new toy. You buy *it*." The word *it* means _____ .

4. Which of the following does this story lead you to believe?
        a. A toy company won't let you buy a toy you like very much.
        b. A toy company takes all your toys away to fix them.
        c. A toy company keeps trying to make toys you will like.

5. What happens when your parent goes to the store? (Which sentence is exactly like the one in your book?)
        a. Your parent looks at toys on TV.
        b. Your parent runs the country.
        c. Your parent picks up a box of cereal.

6. The main idea of the whole story is that
        a. we can buy all our cereals in a store.
        b. we can vote for or against something.
        c. your vote is not important.

7. The opposite of *against* (paragraph two, sentence five) is _____ .

Old Ways and New Pots

1   Grandmother lives in a pueblo. The pueblo is high on a mesa. Grandmother's house is made of mud bricks, called adobe. It has a dirt floor. The house has no water, so Grandmother gets water from a well close by. Grandmother likes living in the pueblo. She likes to see the sun and the sky. At the pueblo she can follow the old ways.

2   The people of the pueblo make clay pots. In the old days, the pots were used every day. They held food, water, or seeds. Now people come from far away to buy them. The pots are thin and beautiful.

3   Some of Grandmother's children moved to the city. Then their lives changed. Her grand-daughter Jackie rides a bike to school. At night she does her homework and watches TV.

4   Sometimes Jackie visits her grandmother. She hears stories of the old days. She learns how to make pots. Jackie's pots are thick and lumpy. Often she has to start over. Her grandmother says, "Keep trying. One day your pots will be beautiful, too!"

1. The people of the pueblo make

    a. bicycles.　b. books.　c. pots.　d. clay.

2. The word in the story that means *a high flat place* is

    _____.

3. The story says, "Grandmother likes living in the pueblo. She likes to see the sun and the sky." The word *she* means _____.

4. Which of the following does this story lead you to believe?

    a. The people of the pueblo don't make good pots.

    b. Jackie will learn to make beautiful pots.

    c. The people of the city stay away from the pueblo.

5. How were the pots used? (Which sentence is exactly like the one in your book?)

    a. They were used to water plants.

    b. They held mud bricks.

    c. They held food, water, or seeds.

6. The main idea of the whole story is that

    a. Jackie is learning old ways and new ways.

    b. Jackie's pots are not good.

    c. Jackie likes to watch TV.

7. The opposite of *low* (paragraph one, second sentence) is

    _____.

The Tree That Was Always Different

A man and his four children lived in a hot country. Here the trees were always green. One day, the man and his children moved to a different land. This land had four seasons. Soon after they came, the four children heard about a beautiful tree. It was called the redbud. Each child wanted very much to see this tree.

One day in early spring, the man went to the woods. The oldest son went, too. "Father," he said, "where is the redbud?"

"There," said the father. The oldest son was surprised. The tree had no leaves! He wondered why it was called a redbud. But he did not ask.

In late spring, the father showed the oldest daughter the redbud. It was bright with many flowers.

"How beautiful it is!" the daughter cried.

In early summer, the third child went with his father to the woods. "Look!" said the father. "There is the redbud!"

"It is just a tree with green leaves," the third child thought. "I wonder why it is called a redbud." But he did not ask.

51

At last, in the fall, the youngest daughter went to the woods. "Father," she said, "show me the redbud."

"There," said the father.

"It is just a tree with leaves and little bean pods," the youngest child thought. She wondered why it was called a redbud. "If I ask, my father will think I know nothing." So she kept quiet. But as soon as she was home, she ran to the others. "I have seen the redbud," she said. "It is not beautiful. It just has leaves and bean pods."

"That is not the redbud," the oldest son said. "The redbud has no leaves."

"What?" cried the second son. "Of course it has leaves. But it does not have bean pods."

"Bean pods? What tree have you seen?" asked the oldest daughter. "The redbud is covered with beautiful flowers."

Just then the father came up to them. He was laughing. "You have all seen the same tree. But you have seen it at different times. In early spring, the redbud has no leaves. Then it has beautiful flowers. After the flowers fall, the leaves come out. Now it has bean pods."

The children looked at each other. They laughed, too. "We were all right. And we were all wrong," the oldest brother said. "We have learned one thing! There is more than one way to look at something!"

409 words

Living Up High

1   Some people live in high mountains. The air up high is thin. Mountain people are used to the thin air. They feel good when they live up high.

2   Most people live in low places. If they go up high, they sometimes feel dizzy and sick. They have to breathe faster. Their hearts beat faster. They have to move slowly. If they stay up high for a long time, their bodies will change. Their lungs will become large. Their larger lungs will help them to breathe the thin air.

3   Airplanes fly high over the mountains. Big planes have extra air so the people inside don't get dizzy. The air gets thinner as you go higher. Out in space there is no air at all.

4   In Colombia, South America, most people live far up on the mountains. Sometimes they go down to the low country. People living there feel fine. But the people from the mountains feel sick.

1. People who go up high in the mountains often get
    a. hot.   b. sleepy.   c. dizzy.   d. fat.

2. The word in the story that means *the body parts you use to breathe*
   is _____.

3. The story says, "Most people live in low places. If *they* go up high,
   they sometimes feel dizzy and sick." The word *they* means

   _____.

4. Which of the following does this story lead you to believe?
    a. People get used to the air where they live.
    b. Air out in space is thin.
    c. People in spaceships don't breathe.

5. What happens to people when they go up high? (Which sentence is
   exactly like the one in the book?)
    a. If they go up high, they feel better.
    b. If they go up high, they sleep better.
    c. If they go up high, they sometimes feel dizzy and sick.

6. The main idea of the whole story is that
    a. people's bodies change when they go to live in high places.
    b. people in low places get sick.
    c. airplanes fly high to get over the mountains.

7. The opposite of *well* (paragraph two, sentence two) is

   _____.

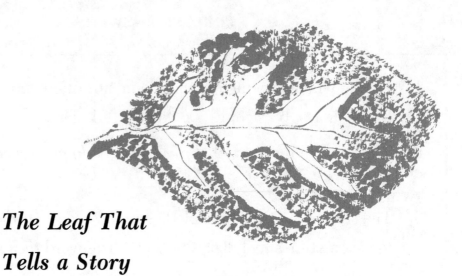

The Leaf That Tells a Story

1   A hundred million years ago, a leaf fell to the ground. It landed in soft mud. More mud covered the leaf. After a long time the mud dried. Rocks and water pressed down on it.

2   Years passed. The dirt around the leaf was pressed to stone. The leaf became dust. But it had left a mark on the stone. The mark was shaped like the leaf. It was a fossil.

3   There are many kinds of fossils. Sometimes a whole animal became a fossil. Some fossils are shaped like fish. Some are shaped like birds.

4   Today, scientists look at the fossils. From the fossils, scientists can learn what kind of trees grew long ago. They can tell what kind of animals once lived on earth.

5   Fossils can be found in many places. Look at the rocks you pick up. You may find a fossil. It may be one hundred million years old!

1. By looking at fossils, scientists can learn about
   a. long ago.   c. stones.
   b. tomorrow.   d. water.

2. The word in the story that means *fell to the ground* is

   _____ .

3. The story says, "You may find a fossil. *It* may be one hundred

   million years old!" The word *it* means _____ .

4. Which of the following does the story lead you to believe?
   a. Fossils are shaped like people, birds, and animals.
   b. Fossils tell us what the earth was like long ago.
   c. Fossils are always hard to find.

5. What can fossils tell us? (Which sentence is exactly like the
   one in your book?)
   a. They can tell us which animals people ate.
   b. They can tell us how many animals lived on the earth.
   c. They can tell what kind of animals once lived on earth.

6. The main idea of the whole story is that
   a. fossils tell a story about the earth.
   b. you can pick up rocks in many places.
   c. scientists cannot learn anything from fossils.

7. The opposite of *died* (paragraph four, sentence three) is

   _____ .

The Fish on the Mountain

1   It is no surprise to find seashells in the sand. Most seashells are found near the sea. But some seashells have been found on high mountaintops. That is a funny place for seashells. How did they get there?

2   The earth did not always look the way it does today. Once the sea covered more of the land. Then mountains pushed up. They pushed up through the water. Land from the bottom of the sea became mountaintops. Seashells and fish bones were pushed up, too. They were far away from sea water. They were left high and dry.

3   The seashells and fish bones were covered with soft mud and sand. The mud became hard. It turned to stone. The shapes of the shell and bones were pressed into the stone. These stones are called fossils.

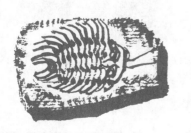

4   Fossils have been found all over our country. Have you ever found one?

1. Some seashells have been found
   a. in trees.
   c. on roads.
   b. on mountaintops.
   d. in the air.

2. The word in the story that means *shapes of bones pressed into stone* is _____.

3. The story says, "The earth did not always look the way *it* does today." The word *it* means _____.

4. Which of the following does this story lead you to believe?
   a. Fish began to live in trees.
   b. Fossils can be found far away from the sea.
   c. Seashells turned into fish bones.

5. What happened to seashells and fish bones? (Which sentence is exactly like the one in your book?)
   a. They were left under the water.
   b. Seashells and fish bones were left far from the water.
   c. Seashells and fish bones were pushed up, too.

6. The main idea of the whole story is that
   a. seashells are funny.
   b. mud turns into stone.
   c. the earth has changed.

7. The opposite of *lost* (in paragraph four) is _____.

A River of Ice

1   Snow fell on the mountain. It snowed and snowed. The snow did not melt. It became deep and heavy. The snow on the bottom pressed together. It became ice.

2   The ice was very wide and thick. It began to move down the mountain. It was like a river of ice. It was a glacier.

3   Sometimes the glacier moved only a few inches each day. As it moved, it took rocks and dirt with it. It changed the land. In some places, it left hills. In some places, when the glacier melted, it made rivers and lakes.

4   A million years ago, there were many big glaciers. Glaciers covered many parts of the world. The glaciers changed the land.

5   Glaciers are still at work today. A glacier in the north of Canada is cutting a new path down the side of a mountain. This glacier will change the land, too.

1. The snow that fell on the mountain
   a. became snowmen.   c. melted.
   b. became ice.   d. turned to rain.

2. The word in the story that means *a river of ice* is _____ .

3. The story says, "The snow did not melt. *It* became deep and heavy." The word *it* means _____ .

4. Which of the following does this story lead you to believe?
   a. There are not as many glaciers as there used to be.
   b. Glaciers do not change the land as they move over it.
   c. Glaciers are found only in warm places.

5. How fast did the glacier move? (Which sentence is exactly like the one in your book?)
   a. Sometimes the glacier moved only once a year.
   b. Sometimes the glacier moved over ten miles each day.
   c. Sometimes the glacier moved only a few inches each day.

6. The main idea of the whole story is that
   a. snow is heavy.
   b. the high land never changes.
   c. glaciers changed the land.

7. The opposite of *south* (paragraph five, sentence two) is _____ .

The River That Dug a Canyon

1   The Colorado River has been working for millions of years. It has been digging the Grand Canyon.

2   At first, the water was even with the land on each side. The water raced along. It carried dirt and rocks with it. Each year the water cut away a little more of the land. The river bed became deep. Today the river is at the bottom of the Grand Canyon.

3   Many people visit the Grand Canyon. Some people ride mules down the sides of the canyon. They pass layers of rock cut by the river. The layers are different colors. The colors tell many things. They tell how the land was built up before the river began to cut through it.

4   The Colorado River is still racing along at the bottom of the canyon. It is still digging away at the Grand Canyon.

1. The layers of rock in the Grand Canyon are
    a. mule paths.
    c. different colors.
    b. the river bed.
    d. at the bottom.

2. The word in the story that means *a deep valley* is _____.

3. The story says, "The water raced along. *It* carried dirt and rocks with it." The word *it* means _____.

4. Which of the following does this story lead you to believe?
    a. Years from now the Grand Canyon may be much deeper.
    b. Both people and mules live in the Grand Canyon.
    c. The Grand Canyon is not very deep any more.

5. What is the Colorado River still doing? (Which sentence is exactly like the one in your book?)
    a. It is still flowing along through the Grand Canyon.
    b. It is still turning different colors.
    c. It is still digging away at the Grand Canyon.

6. The main idea of the whole story is that
    a. rocks have colors.
    b. a river dug the Grand Canyon.
    c. mules ride in the Colorado River.

7. The opposite of *after* (paragraph three, sentence six) is

_____.

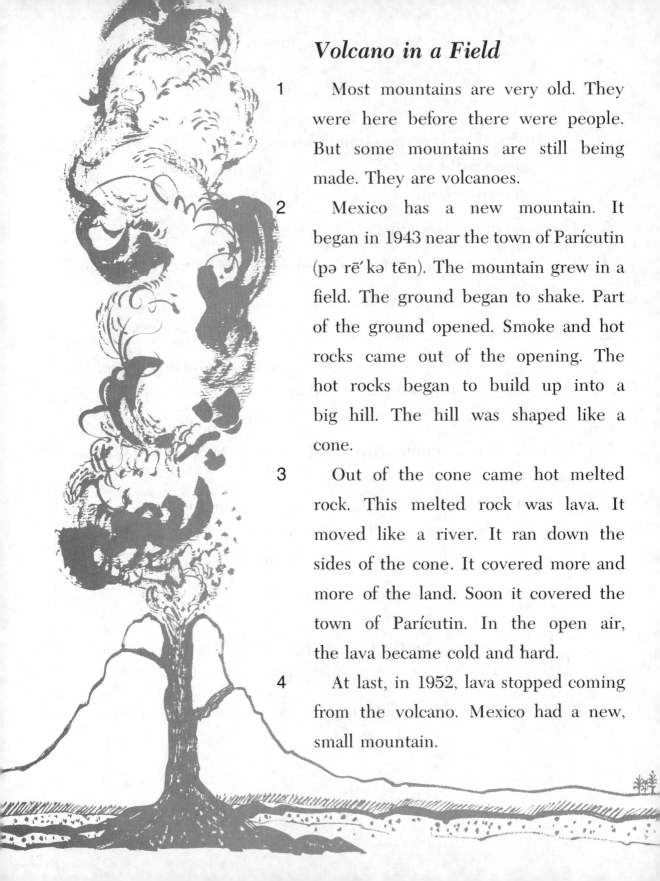

Volcano in a Field

1   Most mountains are very old. They were here before there were people. But some mountains are still being made. They are volcanoes.

2   Mexico has a new mountain. It began in 1943 near the town of Parícutin (pə rē′ kə tēn). The mountain grew in a field. The ground began to shake. Part of the ground opened. Smoke and hot rocks came out of the opening. The hot rocks began to build up into a big hill. The hill was shaped like a cone.

3   Out of the cone came hot melted rock. This melted rock was lava. It moved like a river. It ran down the sides of the cone. It covered more and more of the land. Soon it covered the town of Parícutin. In the open air, the lava became cold and hard.

4   At last, in 1952, lava stopped coming from the volcano. Mexico had a new, small mountain.

1. The new mountain was made
      a. by a river.   c. in Mexico.
      b. by people.   d. in America.

2. The word in the story that means *hot, melted rock* is

   _____ .

3. The story says, "Most mountains are very old. *They* were here before there were people." The word *they* means

   _____ .

4. Which of the following does this story lead you to believe?
      a. Dogs and children liked to play in the hot lava.
      b. Many people in Parícutin had to leave their homes.
      c. The new mountain made the people in town very happy.

5. What happened to the lava in the open air? (Which sentence is exactly like the one in your book?)
      a. In the open air, the lava turned into fish eggs.
      b. In the open air, the lava became cold and hard.
      c. In the open air, the lava turned to rain.

6. The main idea of the whole story is that
      a. new mountains are still being made.
      b. people in Mexico like lava.
      c. people are older than mountains.

7. The opposite of *closed* (paragraph two, sentence five) is

   _____ .

How Cities Began

1   Do you live in a city? Do you know how cities began? Long ago, the world had only a few thousand people. These people moved from place to place. They moved over the land, hunting animals for food.

2   No one knows how or when these people learned about growing food. But when they did, their lives changed. They did not have to look for food any more. They could stay in one place and grow it.

3   People began to live near one another. And so the first villages grew. Many people came to work in the villages. These villages grew very big.

4   When machines came along, life in the villages changed again. Factories were built. More and more people lived near the factories. The cities grew very big.

5   Today, some people are moving back to small towns. Can you tell why?

1. People moved from place to place hunting
   a. animals.   c. machines.
   b. villages.   d. factories.

2. The word in the story that means *found out about something*

   is _____ .

3. The story says, "No one knows how or when these people learned about growing food. But when *they* did, their lives changed."

   The word *they* means _____ .

4. Which of the following does this story lead you to believe?
   a. All people like to live only in very big cities.
   b. It is good to live near a factory.
   c. Some people do not like to live in big cities.

5. What happened when factories were built? (Which sentence is exactly like the one in your book?)
   a. People began to live in the factories.
   b. More and more people lived near the factories.
   c. There are many machines in big city factories.

6. The main idea of the whole story is that
   a. factories were built after the cities grew big.
   b. people like to eat when they visit big cities.
   c. cities began when people lived and worked near each other.

7. The opposite of *to* (in sentence four) is _____ .

A Bag of Bugs

1   When you are sick, you go to a doctor. Where do you go when your tooth hurts? What do you think people did long ago when they were sick?

2   Make believe you are a child of long ago. You are sick. What do you do?

3   Are you coughing? Put a bag of live bugs around your neck. Does your neck hurt? Put pepper on a piece of fat. Now tie the fat around your neck. Do you have warts? Dig a hole in the ground. Put your mother's dishcloth in it. The warts will go away.

4   Does a tooth need pulling? Tie a string around it. Tie one end of the string to a branch of a small tree. Let the branch go. There goes your tooth!

5   These were some things people did long ago when they were sick. Aren't you glad you don't have to wear a bag of bugs?

1. When you are sick, you go to
   a. a store.   c. a baker.
   b. a park.   d. a doctor.

2. The word in the story that means *a cloth used for washing dishes*

   is _____ .

3. The story says, "What do you think people did long ago when *they*

   were sick?" The word *they* means _____ .

4. Which of the following does this story lead you to believe?
   a. A bag of bugs can make you well.
   b. Sick people want to get well.
   c. It's fun to be sick.

5. What could you do if you had a cough? (Which sentence is exactly
   like the one in your book?)
   a. Swing on the branch of a small tree.
   b. Eat fat with pepper on it.
   c. Put a bag of live bugs around your neck.

6. The main idea of the whole story is that
   a. children of long ago liked pepper.
   b. sick people tried many things to get well.
   c. doctors want you to wear bugs around your neck.

7. The opposite of *sad* (paragraph five, sentence two) is _____ .

PUPILLA

VIA

URBS

SAL

VALLUM

Are You a Little Doll?

1   Long ago, people in Rome talked to one another in Latin. Pupils in school learned to read and write Latin. Books were in Latin.

2   Some Romans went to other parts of the world. They took their language with them. Soon Latin was used in many countries. It became a world language.

3   People in other countries did not talk Latin the same way. In each land, they changed the language a little. As time went by, they made more changes. At last they did not speak in Latin any more. New languages had come from the old one.

4   People do not talk to one another in Latin today. But they still use many Latin words. You do, too. *Street, wall, city,* and *salt* are some of the Latin words we use. You are a pupil in school. *Pupil* is a Latin word. It means "little doll."

1. Latin was used by people in
    a. Rome.
    c. the United States.
    b. Greece.
    d. Texas.

2. The word in the story that means *what people speak and write* is _____.

3. The story says, "People do not talk to each other in Latin today. But *they* still use many Latin words." The word *they* means

    _____.

4. Which of the following does this story lead you to believe?
    a. It is not good to change a language.
    b. Pupils in schools today play with dolls.
    c. Not many people can read Latin today.

5. What happened to Latin when it was taken to other countries? (Which sentence is exactly like the one in your book?)
    a. In each land, people talked about each other.
    b. In each land, they changed the language a little.
    c. In each land, the children had to speak some Latin.

6. The main idea of the whole story is that
    a. Romans did not like to stay home.
    b. people in old Rome talked a lot to each other.
    c. Latin changed as it moved from land to land.

7. The opposite of *first* (in paragraph three, sentence four) is

    _____.

Please Pass the Pepper

1   Long ago, some people in Europe went to fight a war. The war was in Asia. These people lost the war. But they came back with many new things.

2   They brought back glass. They brought silk. And they brought back spices. Pepper and cinnamon were some of the spices.

cinnamon

3   People in Asia had used spices for a long time. But before the war in Asia, people in Europe knew nothing about spices. Once they tasted spices on their food, they wanted more. But spices were hard to get. Having lost the war, people could not go to Asia by land. They had to find other ways to get there. They looked for a way to go by sea.

pepper

4   They did not find their way to Asia. But they found something else. They found America. Many people left their own countries. They came to America to live.

5   Because of spices, the lives of some people changed.

1. The war was in
   - a. South America.
   - b. North America.
   - c. Asia.
   - d. the United States.

2. The word in the story that means *pepper and cinnamon* is

   _____.

3. The story says, "Many people left their own countries. *They* came to America to live." The word *they* means _____.

4. Which of the following does this story lead you to believe?
   - a. Looking for one thing may lead to finding something else.
   - b. People cannot live in their own countries.
   - c. People in Europe had known about spices for many years.

5. What happened when the people of Europe tasted spices? (Which sentence is exactly like the one in your book?)
   - a. Once they tasted spices on their food, they wanted more.
   - b. Once they tasted spices, they ate all their food.
   - c. Once they tasted spices, they would not eat.

6. The main idea of the whole story is that
   - a. the people of Europe wanted spices.
   - b. glass and silk are better than spices.
   - c. pepper is hard to get.

7. The opposite of *sea* (paragraph three, sentence five) is

   _____.

Send a Message

1   An American Indian put her ear to the ground. She heard many horses. They were coming her way. She ran to tell her people. Then she ran to tell the people of the next village. She was a runner. Using runners was one way Indians sent messages.

2   People in a land across the sea sent messages, too. One man beat his drum. In the next village the people heard the drum. They beat their drums. The message went from village to village by drums.

3   Much later, some armies kept many pigeons. These pigeons always flew back to their own nesting place. Suppose a soldier was sent far from his own army. He might take a pigeon along. He could tie a message to the bird's leg. He would let the bird go. It would fly home with the soldier's message.

4   These were slow ways to send messages. Can you think of fast ways?

1. When the American Indian listened for horses, she put her ear to
   the   a. tree.   c. table.
                  b. water.   d. ground.

2. The word in the story that means *a person who carries a message* is
   _____.

3. The story says, "An American Indian put her ear to the ground. *She*
   heard many horses." The word *she* means _____.

4. Which of the following does the story lead you to believe?
   a. People have always used pigeons to send messages.
   b. Pigeons like soldiers who send messages.
   c. There are better ways to send messages today.

5. How could a soldier use a pigeon to send a message? (Which
   sentence is exactly like the one in your book?)
   a. He could tie a pigeon to his leg.
   b. He could tie a message to the bird's leg.
   c. He could fly the message home with a pigeon.

6. The main idea of the whole story is that
   a. American Indians run a lot to carry messages.
   b. people like to beat drums to make music.
   c. messages have been sent in many ways.

7. The opposite of *fast* (paragraph four, sentence one) is
   _____.

When Schools Were Different

1   Does your teacher live with you? In pioneer days, a teacher took turns living with each child's family.

2   Sometimes in schools, children did not listen to the teacher. Then they had to wear tall paper hats called dunce caps. Sometimes children had to stand in corners facing the wall. Other times they had to sit in odd places.

3   The teacher had a chair and table. The children sat on log benches. There were no desks. Many times the boys sat on one bench and the girls on another. Children had slates to write on. But sometimes they went to the "writing table." This was a board in one corner of the room. Here, children could write on paper with pen and ink.

4   Pioneer children made their own pens and ink. Pens were made from turkey feathers. The hard part of the feather was made into a point. Ink was made from berries.

5   How different is your school today?

1. Children made pens from
    - a. berries.
    - b. logs.
    - c. turkey feathers.
    - d. sticks.

2. The word in the story that means *hats* is _____ .

3. The story says, "Children had slates to write on. But sometimes *they* went to the 'writing table.'" The word *they* means

    _____ .

4. Which of the following does this story lead you to believe?
    - a. Our schools are better than the pioneer schools.
    - b. It is good to write on slates in schools.
    - c. Boards are kept in corners for children to sit on.

5. What did the children sit on? (Which sentence is exactly like the one in your book?)
    - a. The children sat on log benches.
    - b. The children sat on the writing tables.
    - c. The children sat on the floor.

6. The main idea of the whole story is that
    - a. pioneer children made their own log benches.
    - b. children need turkey feathers to make their own pens.
    - c. pioneer schools were very different from our schools.

7. The opposite of *stand* (paragraph two, sentence four) is _____ .

Gold from Making Pants

1   Many years ago gold was found in California. Some people wanted to get rich. They went to California to find gold. One of those people was a young man named Levi Strauss.

2   Levi took some strong cloth with him. He planned to sell it in California. The cloth would make a good tent. It would make a good wagon cover. When he sold the cloth, he would have money. Then he would mine for gold.

3   But Levi's plan soon changed. In California, he met a miner who said, "Mining is hard work. My pants wear out fast." That gave Levi an idea. He made pants from his cloth. The miner liked the new pants. They didn't wear out.

4   The other miners heard about Levi's pants. He made more pants. Soon all the miners were wearing "Levi's." They paid for the pants with gold. Levi changed his mind about looking for gold. He got gold from making pants.

1. Levi used his cloth to make

   a. tents.   b. wagon covers.   c. hats.   d. pants.

2. The word in the story that means *a person who digs for gold* is

   _____.

3. The story says, "Levi took some strong cloth with him . He planned to sell *it* in California." The word *it* means _____.

4. Which of the following does the story lead you to believe?

   a. All the miners got rich.

   b. Levi got rich.

   c. Mining is fun.

5. Why did people go to California? (Which sentence is exactly like the one in your book?)

   a. They went to California to buy cloth.

   b. They went to California to make tents.

   c. They went to California to find gold.

6. The main idea of the whole story is

   a. plans can change.

   b. mining is hard work.

   c. cloth makes good tents.

7. The opposite of *weak* (paragraph two, sentence one) is

   _____.

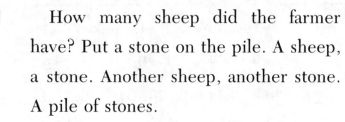

A Stone for a Sheep

1   How many sheep did the farmer have? Put a stone on the pile. A sheep, a stone. Another sheep, another stone. A pile of stones.

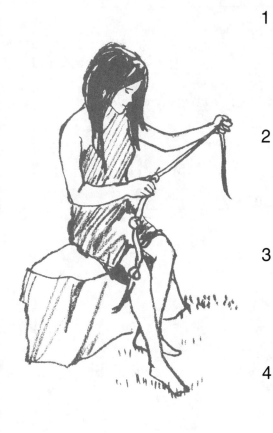

2   How many animals did the hunter kill? Make a cut in a stick. Make a big cut for a lion. Make a small cut for a bird.

3   How many days ago was the seed planted? Tie a knot in a rope each day. One day, one knot. Many days, many knots.

4   Once there were no words for numerals. People could not tell how many. They could match a sheep to a stone. They could match a cut in a stick to each animal. But they could not count.

5   After a while people had a word for one, for two, for three, for many. They counted, "One, two, three, many." More than three were many. Today, we can count any number of things and tell exactly how many.

1. A farmer counted sheep with
   - a. seeds.
   - b. cuts in sticks.
   - c. birds.
   - d. stones.

2. The word in the story that means *1, 2, 3, 4,* and *5* is _____ .

3. The story says, "People could not tell how many. *They* could match a sheep to a stone." The word *they* means _____ .

4. Which of the following does this story lead you to believe?
   - a. Piling stones is the best way to count.
   - b. People can count better with numerals.
   - c. Knots in ropes help seeds grow.

5. What words did people long ago use in counting? (Which sentence is exactly like the one in your book?)
   - a. They counted how many sheep made knots.
   - b. They counted many more than three.
   - c. They counted, "One, two, three, many."

6. The main idea of the whole story is that
   - a. hunters killed animals.
   - b. people learned to count.
   - c. farmers had lots of stones.

7. The opposite of *many* (paragraph three, sentence three) is

   _____ .

The Year the Barn Burned Down

1   Have you ever heard people say, "I remember that. That was the year the cow fell through the ice"? Or "That was the year the barn burned down"?

2   Indians counted years this way. They would draw pictures on animal skins. The pictures named the years that some big thing took place. They might tell of "the fire that killed the animals" summer. Or "the rivers that covered the land" spring.

3   Long ago, years were remembered in different ways. Suppose you lived in ancient Rome. You would count the years from the time Rome began as a city. Suppose you lived in ancient Egypt. You would name the years from the time each ruler began to rule.

4   We count years by numbers, too. Sometimes we put the letters B.C. and A.D. after the year. Why do we do this? Do you know what the letters mean? What do we count our years from?

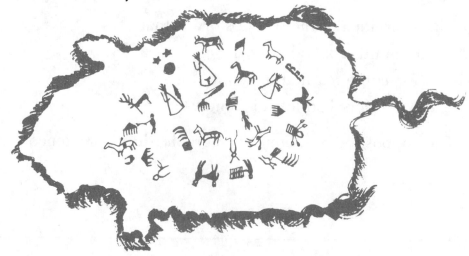

1. The Indians counted years with
    a. pictures.   c. animals.
    b. fire.   d. rivers.

2. The word in the story that means *very old* is _____.

3. The story says, "Indians counted years this way. *They* would draw pictures on animal skins." The word *they* means

    _____ .

4. Which of the following does this story lead you to believe?
    a. Indians had many animals to count.
    b. People in Rome did not know how to count the years.
    c. Keeping count of the years is important to people.

5. How would you count the years if you lived in ancient Rome? (Which sentence is exactly like the one in your book?)
    a. You would count the years from the time Rome began as a city.
    b. You would count the years until you could go to live in Egypt.
    c. You would count the years it would take to leave Rome.

6. The main idea of the whole story is that
    a. Indians drew counting pictures on animal skins.
    b. years have been counted in different ways.
    c. we need kings to tell us how to count.

7. The opposite of *fall* (paragraph two, sentence five) is _____.

The Time of the Falling Leaves

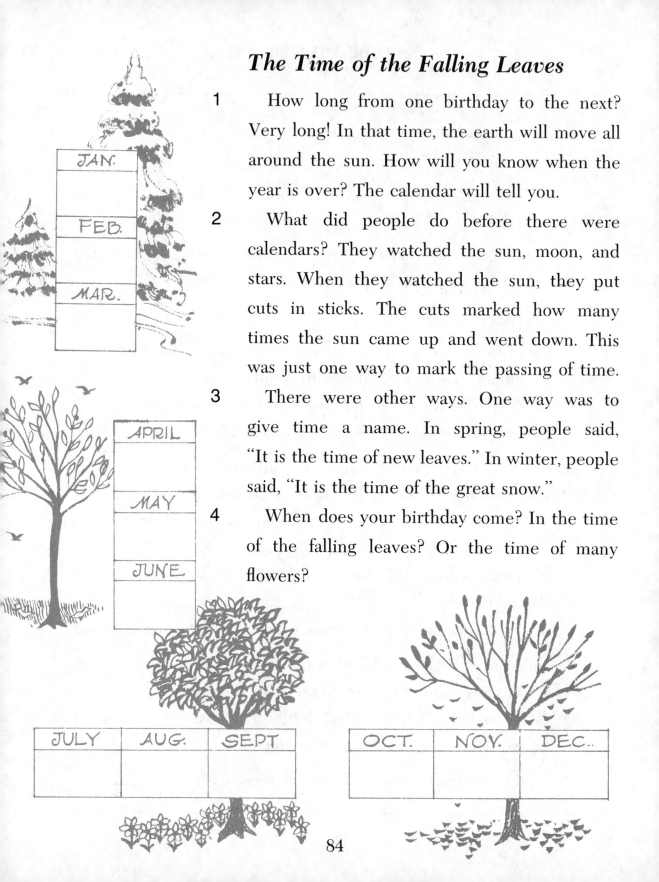

1   How long from one birthday to the next? Very long! In that time, the earth will move all around the sun. How will you know when the year is over? The calendar will tell you.

2   What did people do before there were calendars? They watched the sun, moon, and stars. When they watched the sun, they put cuts in sticks. The cuts marked how many times the sun came up and went down. This was just one way to mark the passing of time.

3   There were other ways. One way was to give time a name. In spring, people said, "It is the time of new leaves." In winter, people said, "It is the time of the great snow."

4   When does your birthday come? In the time of the falling leaves? Or the time of many flowers?

84

1. The time of the new leaves is
    a. winter.
    c. spring.
    b. fall.
    d. sun up.

2. The word in the story that means *the time in which the earth moves all around the sun* is _____.

3. The story says, "In spring, people said, 'It is the time of new leaves.'" The word *it* means _____.

4. Which of the following does this story lead you to believe?
    a. There have not always been calendars.
    b. Your birthday is always on January 1st.
    c. We do not need calendars.

5. When did the people put cuts in sticks? (Which sentence is exactly like the one in your book?)
    a. When the new moon came up, they put cuts in sticks.
    b. When they watched the sun, they put cuts in sticks.
    c. They put cuts in sticks when they watched the sun.

6. The main idea of the whole story is that
    a. people liked to watch the sun go up and come down.
    b. people did not want to use calendars.
    c. people used many ways to mark the passing of time.

7. The opposite of *moon* (paragraph two, sentence two) is _____.

Look for a Sign

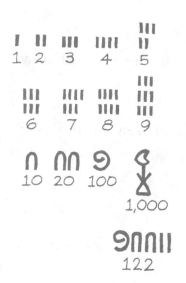

‖	‖	‖‖	‖‖‖	‖‖‖
1	2	3	4	5

1 Long ago, people did not know about numerals. When they wanted to know "how many," they put marks in clay. The Egyptians made a line ǀ for each 1. They used the sign ∩ for 10. For 100, they used still another sign ϐ. Can you tell that this sign ϐ∩ ‖‖‖ is 119? Seem funny? But the Egyptians could count many things with these signs.

2 Other early people also made signs for numerals. They made the signs with a pointed stick in the clay. The signs looked like this ▼ ▼ ▼ . For 10, the mark was turned on its side. The Mayans in South America used dots and lines. They made a dot for 1 like this •. They made a line ____ for five. Nine looked like this ••••. Ten was 2 lines ═══. For 15, they made 3 lines ═══. This was 19 ═══.

3 How old are you? Can you write the answer using Egyptian or Mayan signs?

1. Long ago, people did not know about
   a. clay.
   b. numerals.
   c. lines.
   d. signs.

2. The word in the story that means *lines used for numerals* is

   _____ .

3. The story says, "Other early people also made signs for numerals. *They* made the signs with a pointed stick in the clay." The word

   they means _____ .

4. Which of the following does this story lead you to believe?
   a. It is fun to play with clay.
   b. Pointed sticks were not used to count things.
   c. People long ago made up their own ways to count.

5. How did the Mayans make five? (Which sentence is exactly like the one in your book?)
   a. They made a dot · for five.
   b. They made a line ___ for five.
   c. They used sticks made out of clay for five.

6. The main idea of the whole story is that
   a. Egyptians liked to make clay shapes and numbers.
   b. people used different signs for numerals.
   c. people made pointed sticks.

7. The opposite of *young* (paragraph three, sentence one) is

   _____ .

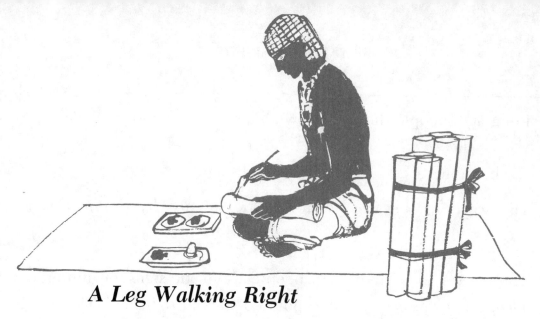

A Leg Walking Right

1   Here are some signs $+ - \div \times$. The signs are very different. They mean very different things. When you see them, you know what to do. This sign $+$ means that you will add some numerals. This sign $-$ means that you will take one numeral away from another. You will subtract. What will you do when you see $\times$ and $\div$?

2   Our signs are easy signs to read. They are easy signs to remember. Look at these two signs 𝈪𝈪. The ancient Egyptians used these signs. A picture of a leg walking to the left 𝈪 told them to add some numerals. A picture of a leg walking to the right 𝈪 told them to subtract.

3   In the 1500s, people used this printed sign & to add numerals. After a while, the sign began to look like this ✝. Later, the sign became $+$.

4   How much is 2 𝈪 2?

1. What do you do when you see this sign **+** ?
    a. Walk away.   c. Write a numeral.
    b. Read a sign.   d. Add.

2. The word in the story that means *to take one numeral away from another* is _____ .

3. The story says, "Our signs are easy signs to read. *They* are easy signs to remember." The word *they* means _____ .

4. Which of the following does this story lead you to believe?
    a. Egyptians could not add numerals together.
    b. All Egyptians had two left legs.
    c. Our signs are not hard to understand.

5. What did the sign to add numerals begin to look like? (Which sentence is exactly like the one in your book?)
    a. After a while, the sign began to look like this **ϯ**.
    b. After a while, the sign began to look like this **+** .
    c. After a while, the sign began to look like this **&**.

6. The main idea of the whole story is that
    a. the signs for adding and subtracting have changed.
    b. people could not write in the 1500s.
    c. the old signs were good for Egyptians but not for us.

7. The opposite of *right* (paragraph two, sentence five) is _____ .

How the Rabbit Got Its Shape

The children sat down near their grandfather. They wanted a story. "The rabbit is funny," they said. "How did it get that way?"

"Rabbit is funny now," said their grandfather. "But long ago, Rabbit was different. It had a long, bushy tail. It was round and fat. Its legs were straight and strong. It walked and ran the way other animals do." And Grandfather told the children this story.

One day, when Rabbit was in the woods, it met a child. The child's name was Little Fox. Little Fox was crying because she was lost. She could not find her way home.

"Do not cry," Rabbit said. "I will take you home." As they walked through the woods, Little Fox fell into a deep hole. "I will get you out," said Rabbit. It put its long, bushy tail down into the hole. Little Fox pulled on the tail. She pulled so hard Rabbit's tail broke off.

Next, Rabbit put its front legs around a tree. It put its back legs into the hole. Little Fox held on to Rabbit's legs with both hands. She pulled and pulled. Rabbit's legs began to stretch. Its fat body grew thin.

At last, Little Fox was out of the hole. Rabbit and Little Fox walked on through the woods. But now Rabbit could not walk on its long back legs. It had to hop.

At last, they came to the house of Little Fox. Little Fox was happy. But Rabbit was not.

"How can I go home?" Rabbit said. "I look so funny."

"Do not be afraid to go home," said Little Fox. "From now on, all rabbits will look like you."

Grandfather looked at the children. "Now you know," he said, "how rabbits got their shape."

275 words

II

Some Changes Are Fast; Some Changes Are Slow

In this section, you will read about things that change very fast and other things that change very slowly. You will read about changes from the standpoint of history, Earth science, arithmetic, biology, economics, and anthropology.

Keep these questions in mind when you are reading.

1. Why do some things change fast and others change slowly?
2. What kind of things change slowly?
3. What kind of things change fast?
4. What things can you think of that cause change to happen?

Look on pages 9-12 for help with words you don't understand in this section.

93

Smoke and Fire

1   When we smell smoke, we think "fire," and fire is a scary thing. Fire can harm things, but it can also help nature.

2   In 1988, Yellowstone Park had some very bad fires. They burned all summer. Firefighters worked hard to put them out, but the fires were too big. They moved too fast. The fires burned until fall, when snow finally put them out.

3   Because many trees and much grass burned, the fires changed the land. Soil washed away, and some animals were killed.

4   But now, good things are happening in Yellowstone. There are more things for the animals to eat. Flowers, berries, and grass grow where the fires burned the trees. The deer and elk like the good grass. Bears like the berries. Dead trees make good homes for bugs and birds. New trees are growing.

Yellowstone is not like it was in 1988. But it is still a good place for animals to live.

1. In 1988 Yellowstone had big
   a. floods. b. rains. c. flowers. d. fires.

2. The word in the story that means *dirt* is _____.

3. The story says, "Fire can harm things, but *it* can also help nature."
   The word *it* means _____.

4. Which of the following does the story lead you to believe?
   a. The firefighters didn't know how to put out fires.
   b. All the animals left and never came back.
   c. Animals like Yellowstone Park.

5. What put the fires out? (Which sentence is exactly like the one in
   your book?)
   a. Firefighters put the fires out.
   b. Rain put the fires out.
   c. The fires burned until fall, when snow finally put them out.

6. The main idea of the whole story is that
   a. the fires changed Yellowstone Park.
   b. there are more bears in Yellowstone Park.
   c. the trees in Yellowstone Park are gone.

7. The opposite of *bad* (paragraph four, sentence one) is
   _____.

Birds Are Better

1   It was summer in a small town in Illinois, and it was hot. Insects were all around. They were outside! They were inside! They bit people! They crawled on food! The people didn't know what to do.

2   Some people wanted to kill the insects with sprays. Others said, "Insect spray will harm the birds and the butterflies. That is a bad idea."

3   Someone said, "Birds can help. Purple martins eat insects. We need purple martins." The people made bird houses and put them along the streets. Soon purple martins built nests in the bird houses. They had baby birds and fed them insects. As the babies got bigger, they ate more and more.

4   The people of the town were happy. They had found a good way to get rid of the insects and not harm the birds and the butterflies. Now there are bird houses in many places and hardly any more insects in the town.

1. The people tried to get rid of
       a. butterflies. b. insects. c. birds. d. purple martins.

2. The word in the story that means *tiny animals with six legs* is

   _____.

3. The story says, "The people made bird houses. *They* put the houses along the streets." The word *they* means _____.

4. Which of the following does the story lead you to believe?
       a. Insect sprays turn birds purple.
       b. Insect sprays can be harmful to birds.
       c. Insect sprays help butterflies.

5. What kind of birds came to the bird houses? (Which sentence in the story is exactly like the one in your book?)
       a. Soon robins came to the bird houses.
       b. Soon bluebirds built nests in the bird houses.
       c. Soon purple martins built nests in the bird houses.

6. The main idea of the whole story is that
       a. butterflies like to be sprayed.
       b. birds are better than sprays to get rid of insects.
       c. the people in Illinois like to make bird houses.

7. The opposite of *cold* (paragraph 1, sentence two) is

   _____.

Animal Skin Ball

1   Some Native Americans were making toys for their children. They made a bow and arrow. They put animal skin around rock and made a ball.

2   Children have played with toys for thousands of years. Once toys were made by hand. They were made from bones or wood or clay. Other things were used, too. People used what they had to make toys. You can still get bows and arrows and balls. But today, these things are made by machines.

3   When toys were made by hand, children did not have many toys. Because they had few toys, children kept them a long time.

4   Have you ever been to a museum? A museum is a building in which old things are kept. Some museums have a room for old toys. Today's toys may be kept in a museum someday.

98

1. The Native Americans were making

   a. museums.   c. machines.

   b. toys.   d. houses.

2. The word in the story that means *a building in which old things are kept* is _____.

3. The story says, "Some Native Americans were making toys for their children. *They* made a bow and arrow." The word *they* means

   _____.

4. Which of the following does the story lead you to believe?

   a. Children had to take good care of their toys long ago.

   b. Long ago, children played with old toys in museums.

   c. A rock covered with animal skin makes a good ball.

5. How were toys made long ago? (Which sentence in the story is exactly like the one in your book?)

   a. They were made from bones or wood or clay.

   b. They were made from stones or mud or hay.

   c. They were made by Native Americans who had children.

6. The main idea of the whole story is that

   a. long ago, toys were made by hand.

   b. today animal skins are kept in museums.

   c. long ago, machines made toys for Indian children.

7. The opposite of *machine* (paragraph two, sentence two) is

   _____.

A Fast Worker

1   The computer is a machine that works very fast. It can add numbers much faster than a person can. It can remember better than a person. It can do many other things. In school a computer can do math. It can help boys and girls read, write, and spell. It can remember the names of all the students in the school.

2   Computers help people drive cars and fly planes. A spaceship needs many computers. Telephones and televisions use computers, too. Some computers, called fax machines, can send letters. The letters travel very fast.

3   A computer can remember what is in a store. It knows all the prices. It tells you how much to pay. It gives you change. Computers can play games, too. A computer named Big Blue is very good at chess. It beat the best chess player in the world.

4   Computers are changing the way we live.

1. A computer is a kind of

   a. toy.   b. animal.   c. machine.   d. person.

2. The word in the story that means *how much money things cost* is

   _____.

3. The story says, "A computer can remember what is in a store. *It* knows all the prices." The word *it* means _____.

4. Which of the following does the story lead you to believe?

   a. Computers make many mistakes.

   b. Computers help people work better and faster.

   c. Schools don't have computers.

5. What do computers do? (Which sentence is exactly like the one in your book?)

   a. Computers remember what you do in school.

   b. Computers help people drive cars and fly planes.

   c. Computers tell you what to buy.

6. The main idea of the whole story is

   a. boys and girls play games in school.

   b. a computer can drive your car.

   c. computers can do many things.

7. The opposite of *forget* (paragraph one, sentence three) is

   _____.

Signs in the Desert

1   The nomads walked in the desert. It was hot and dry. The people of the tribe needed water. Soon some of the tribe called out. They had seen a few small plants. The plants were a sign. Under the plants they would find a little water. The people began to dig. When they found water, they were very happy. They filled their water bags.

2   Other nomads walked in a desert. They, too, needed water. But they looked for a different sign. They followed a long pipeline. The pipeline carried gas across the desert. The gas company had put in water at some places near the pipeline. These desert people knew they would have water when it was needed.

3   There were signs in the desert for both people. But one followed an old sign. The other followed a new sign.

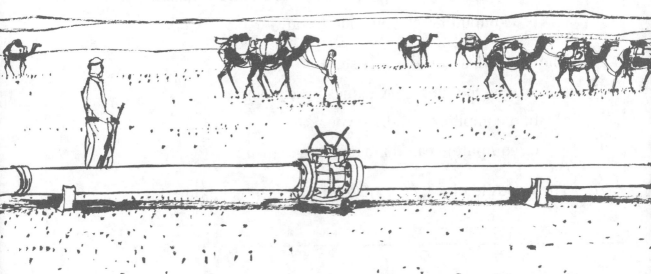

1. The nomads needed
   a. more sun.
   c. bags.
   b. water.
   d. a pipeline.

2. The word in the story that means *people who travel from place to place looking for food and water* is _____ .

3. The story says, "The nomads walked in the desert. *It* was hot and dry." The word *it* means _____ .

4. Which of the following does this story lead you to believe?
   a. Nomads like to walk in the desert.
   b. Nomads are always happy.
   c. People cannot live without water.

5. What did the pipeline carry? (Which sentence is exactly like the one in your book?)
   a. The pipeline carried the people to the desert.
   b. The pipeline carried water to the gas company.
   c. The pipeline carried gas across the desert.

6. The main idea of the whole story is that
   a. desert people followed different signs to find water.
   b. gas companies put signs on plants in the desert.
   c. the desert people liked to dig up desert plants.

7. The opposite of *lost* (in sentence nine) is _____ .

Kings and Queens of Candy

1   Once candy was not made for children. In one country, almost 5,000 years ago, candy was made only for the rulers. Today, children are the kings and queens of candy.

2   Do you ever eat licorice? People in ancient times ate licorice, too. They did not think of licorice as candy at first. They ate licorice to keep them strong and well. In some countries, people ate licorice to make them beautiful! Later, people ate it just because it tasted good.

3   All candy was made by hand until 1845. In that year, someone made a candy machine. Soon other candy machines were made. At first, not much candy was sold. But by the 1900s, candy was sold all over the world. Today, candy companies say people eat from 20 to 30 pounds of candy a year. More than 2,000 different kinds of candy are made!

4   How many kinds of candy do you eat, your majesty?

1. Candy was first made for
   a. children
   b. animals.
   c. rulers.
   d. companies.

2. A word in the story that means *persons who rule over many people* is _____ .

3. The story says, "People in ancient times ate licorice, too. *They* did not think of licorice as candy at first." The word *they* means

   _____ .

4. Which of the following does this story lead you to believe?
   a. Today people eat licorice to make their hair grow.
   b. Today people eat licorice because ancient people ate it.
   c. Today people eat licorice because they like it.

5. How many kinds of candy are there? (Which sentence is exactly like the one in your book?)
   a. Not enough kinds of candy are made.
   b. More than 2,000 different kinds of candy are made!
   c. Different kinds of companies make many kinds of candy.

6. The main idea of the whole story is that
   a. candy companies think people eat too much candy.
   b. people have liked candy since ancient times.
   c. licorice will make you grow big and strong.

7. The opposite of *modern* (sentence five) is _____ .

The Cat and the Clover

1   A man and woman looked at their field. Once it had been covered with red clover. This plant made good feed for their cows. But now most of the clover was gone. The farmers wanted more red clover in their fields. So they got a cat.

2   The cat hunted for field mice. For years, field mice had been tearing down bumblebee nests. Once bumblebees had carried pollen from one clover to another. Now most of the bumblebees were gone. Without bumblebees to carry the pollen, most of the clover died.

3   The cat killed the mice. Soon there were no mice left. Now other bumblebees began to make new nests. The bumblebees flew over the field. They carried the pollen from clover to clover again.

4   The following year, the man and woman looked at their field. It was covered with red clover. After that, they always kept a cat.

106

1. The farmers' field had once been covered with
   - a. red clover.
   - b. field mice.
   - c. bumblebees.
   - d. grass.

2. The word in the story that means *the fine yellow dust in the flower of the clover* is _____ .

3. The story says, "The man and woman looked at their field. Once *it* had been covered with red clover." The word *it* means_____ .

4. Which of the following does this story lead you to believe?
   - a. Some field mice help farmers to grow better crops.
   - b. Some insects and animals are of great help to us.
   - c. Cats like to play in clover.

5. What did the cat do? (Which sentence is exactly like the one in your book?)
   - a. The cat hunted for bumblebees.
   - b. The cat played in the red clover.
   - c. The cat hunted for field mice.

6. The main idea of the whole story is that
   - a. the cat and the bumblebees helped the farmers.
   - b. cats like cows that eat red clover.
   - c. bumblebees make honey from red clover only.

7. The opposite of *stopped* (paragraph three, sentence three) is _____ .

Desert Rain

1   The desert is a hot, dry place. The sun shines almost every day. For weeks and weeks it does not rain. But plants and animals can still live there.

2   The cactus is a kind of desert plant. Cactus plants can go a long time with no water. They store water in their stems. They use this water in the dry times. Then they get very thin. Desert trees have tiny leaves. They drop the leaves when it is hot and dry. This helps them save water.

3   The packrat gets water from its food. So does the lizard. They never drink. If it's hot, the packrat stays in its den. The lizard hides under a rock.

4   Sometimes it rains in the desert. Then the cactus plants fill up with water. They get fat. Trees make new leaves. The packrat comes out of its den. It eats the fat cactus. The lizard sits on its rock and eats bugs. Rain quickly changes the desert.

1. The cactus is a desert

    a. tree.   b. rat.   c. lizard.   d. plant.

2. The word in the story that means *hot, dry place* is

    _____.

3. The story says, "The packrat comes out of its den. *It* eats the fat cactus." The word *it* means _____.

4. Which of the following does the story lead you to believe?

    a. It never rains in the desert.

    b. Rain hurts desert plants.

    c. Rain helps desert plants grow.

5. What does the packrat do? (Which sentence is exactly like the one in your book?)

    a. If it's hot, the packrat stays in its den.

    b. If it's hot, the packrat gets a drink.

    c. If it's hot, the packrat eats cactus.

6. The main idea of the whole story is that

    a. packrats eat lizards.

    b. lizards don't like sun.

    c. rain changes the desert.

7. The opposite of *wet* (paragraph one, sentence one) is

    _____.

Before There Were Birds

1   Insects have lived on earth for millions of years. They lived on earth before there were birds. They lived on earth before there were dinosaurs.

2   Dinosaurs were big animals. One kind of dinosaur was over 70 feet long. Some insects were big, too. The dragonfly was one foot long. Its wings were more than three feet wide. But most insects were small.

3   While the dinosaurs lived, the earth began to change. New mountains pushed up. The weather changed. In some places, there was not much water. Without water, plants could not live. The dinosaurs could not find food or water. The insects did not need much food and water. And they could fly. They could leave one place and fly to another. The dinosaurs died. But the insects lived. They became very small.

4   Today, there are more insects on earth than any other living thing.

FIND THE ANSWERS

1. Most insects were
    - a. big.
    - b. small.
    - c. fat.
    - d. thin.

2. The word in the story that means *go away* is _____ .

3. The story says, "But the insects lived. *They* became very small."

    The word *they* means _____ .

4. Which of the following does this story lead you to believe?
    - a. There was too much water.
    - b. Dragonflies became bigger than dinosaurs.
    - c. Some animals changed as the earth changed.

5. How could insects find food and water? (Which sentence is exactly like the one in your book?)
    - a. They could follow the dinosaurs to find water.
    - b. They could eat the dinosaurs' food.
    - c. They could leave one place and fly to another.

6. The main idea of the whole story is that
    - a. there are no insects today.
    - b. dinosaurs did not need much food or water.
    - c. insects are the oldest animals on earth.

7. The opposite of *pulled* (paragraph three, sentence two) is

    _____ .

Learning About Chimps

1   Chimpanzees live in Africa. Jane Goodall wanted to learn about wild chimps. She went to live in a jungle camp near the homes of the chimps. She began to study them. The chimps were very shy. They were afraid of people.

2   Jane waited and waited. She waited many months. At last the chimps came close to her. She fed them bananas. The chimps were ready to be friends. The chimps learned to trust Jane. She learned many things about chimps. She learned that they act very much as we do. They use sticks for tools. They even hug and kiss like people do.

3   Jane Goodall studied chimps for 35 years. Today she travels around the world telling people about these animals. She wants people to stop putting chimps in cages. She says they are not happy in cages. Chimpanzees want to be wild and free.

1. Wild chimps

      a. are mean.   c. use tools.

      b. eat peanut butter.   d. like the zoo.

2. The word in the story that means *to be scared* is _____.

3. The story says, "At last the chimps came close to her. She fed *them* bananas." The word *them* means _____.

4. Which of the following does this story lead you to believe?

      a. All chimps live in the zoo.

      b. Chimps like peanut butter.

      c. Chimps are smart.

5. How did the chimps act? (Which sentence is exactly like the one in your book?)

      a. The chimps were very happy.

      b. The chimps were very sad.

      c. The chimps were very shy.

6. The main idea of the whole story is that

      a. Jane Goodall spent a long time learning about chimps.

      b. Jane Goodall likes to travel around the world.

      c. Jane Goodall spent 35 years telling people about chimps.

7. The opposite of *tame* (paragraph one, sentence two) is

   _____.

Plants That Cure

1   Long ago in Egypt, a queen named Hatshepsut started a search for special plants. She believed that the right plants could help to make sick people well.

2   Today in the jungles there are special hunters. They are not hunting animals. They are looking for plants for medicine.

3   These hunters are scientists. They are men and women who work very hard. They go miles and miles into the jungle rain forest. It is very hot and wet. Many strange plants grow there. Some of the plants grow to giant size.

4   Sometimes very plain plants in the city can help sick people. Even plants like daffodils and buttercups can be used for medicine.

1. The plant hunters are
   a. Egyptian queens.   c. hot and wet.
   b. scientists.   d. sick.

2. The word in the story that means *people who work in and study a science* is _____ .

3. The story says, "These hunters are scientists. *They* are men and women who work very hard." The word *they* means _____ .

4. Which of the following does this story lead you to believe?
   a. Sick people like big plants.
   b. Plants are too hot in the jungle rain forest.
   c. The jungle is a good place for plants to grow.

5. What is it like in the jungle rain forest? (Which sentence is exactly like the one in your book?)
   a. Buttercups grow in the jungle rain forest.
   b. There are many scientists there.
   c. It is very hot and wet.

6. The main idea of the whole story is that
   a. scientists can use plants to make medicines.
   b. eating plants makes you sick.
   c. you should grow your own plants.

7. The opposite of *fancy* (in paragraph four, sentence one) is

   _____ .

Does Your Skin Fit?

1   How does your skin fit? Is it big enough for you? Of course it is. Your skin is the outside covering of your body. It grows with you.

2   Have you ever seen a locust? The covering of this insect does not grow. As the locust gets big, its old skin gets too tight. The locust comes out. It leaves its brown skin behind. The skin looks something like an empty shell.

3   As the locust keeps growing, it keeps changing its skin. The locust changes its skin as much as five times, sometimes more.

4   Like all insects, the locust comes from an egg. Most insects look like worms at first. The locust is different. The young locust never looks like a worm. Right away, it looks like a small locust.

5   Next time you see a shell, look at it carefully. It may be the skin some locust left behind.

1. The covering of a locust
   - a. grows.
   - b. gets too tight.
   - c. is yellow.
   - d. looks like a worm.

2. The word in the story that means *not the same* is

   _____ .

3. The story says, "The locust comes out. *It* leaves its brown skin behind." The word *it* means _____ .

4. Which of the following does this story lead you to believe?
   - a. Each new skin of the locust is larger.
   - b. Locusts do not grow very much in size.
   - c. Big locusts live in empty shells.

5. What does the young locust look like? (Which sentence is exactly like the one in your book?)
   - a. The young locust looks like a shell.
   - b. Right away, it looks like a brown worm.
   - c. Right away, it looks like a small locust.

6. The main idea of the whole story is that
   - a. your skin does not fit you.
   - b. locust shells look like worms.
   - c. the locust changes its skin.

7. The opposite of *full* (paragraph two, sentence six) is _____ .

Rivers at Work

1   The Colorado and the Mississippi are both long rivers. They have been working for millions of years. The Colorado River helped make the Grand Canyon. It has cut away more than 5,000 feet of rock. In the same time, the Mississippi River was working, too. It made a wide valley. But it washed away only 150 feet of rock.

2   The Mississippi is a slow river. Slow rivers are wide. When heavy rains fall, the rivers become even wider. Often they flood the towns on their banks. They carry dirt and mud to the ocean. The land around them is fertile. It takes slow rivers a long time to change the land.

3   The Colorado is a fast river. Fast rivers are not wide. The water races along. Sometimes the water falls over high rocks. This is called a waterfall. Fast river water can be used to make electricity. It does not take a fast river long to change the land.

1. The Mississippi River made a

      a. deep canyon.   c. high waterfall.

      b. wide valley.   d. big lake.

2. The word in the story that means *moves very fast* is

      _____.

3. The story says, "When heavy rains fall, the rivers become even wider. Often *they* flood the towns on their banks." The word *they* means _____.

4. Which of the following does this story lead you to believe?

      a. Different rivers change the land in different ways.

      b. Only slow rivers can change the land.

      c. Rivers have to be wide and deep in order to change the land.

5. What do we know about the Colorado River? (Which sentence is exactly like the one in your book?)

      a. The fast Colorado River cut away many feet of hard rock.

      b. The Colorado River helped make the Grand Canyon.

      c. The Colorado River is wide and fast.

6. The main idea of the whole story is that

      a. rivers change the land.

      b. rivers are full of mud.

      c. water can fall over rocks.

7. The opposite of *climbs* (paragraph three, sentence four) is

      _____.

Bells on Your Ears

1   Suppose the children in your school start wearing bells on their ears. You laugh. It is funny. But what happens when most of the children in the country start wearing bells on their ears, too? Now it seems the right thing to do. It is the style.

2   In early America, men used to wear wigs. Men in other countries also had wigs. It was the style.

3   People have always tried to color and shape the things around them. This is what we call style.

4   There are styles in many things. There are styles in music. There are styles in gardens. There are styles in painting. Some styles change a little. Some styles change very much. Some styles stay the same.

5   Think of some of the styles we have today. Do you think they will seem funny many years from now?

1. When most of the children in the country wear bells on their ears it is
   - a. funny.
   - b. silly.
   - c. wrong.
   - d. the style.

2. The word in the story that means *coverings of hair to wear over your own hair* is _____ .

3. The story says, "Think of some of the styles we have today. Do you think *they* will seem funny many years from now?" The word *they* means _____ .

4. Which of the following does this story lead you to believe?
   - a. Our styles may seem funny to people from other lands.
   - b. We don't know what the style was in early America.
   - c. People in other countries should wear wigs today.

5. What did men in early America do? (Which sentence is exactly like the one in your book?)
   - a. In early America, the men were in style.
   - b. The men wore wigs in early America.
   - c. In early America, men used to wear wigs.

6. The main idea of the whole story is that
   - a. there are styles in many things.
   - b. only men wear wigs.
   - c. music is all right for some people.

7. The opposite of *cry* (in sentence two) is _____ .

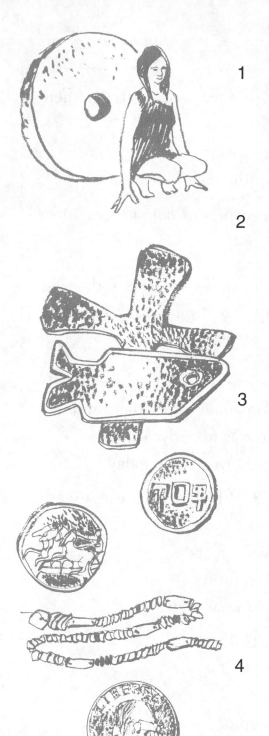

Stone Money, Feather Money

1   I want something you have. You want something I have. Sometimes I give you money. Sometimes you give me money. It can be metal money. It can be paper money.

2   What kind of money did people have long ago? Some people used stones as money. Others used feathers. Many people used animals. Later, gold came into use as money. But this money was hard to carry. It was heavy.

3   Some people thought of making metals in special shapes. Each special shape would be worth something different. In some places, people shaped the gold to look like animals. They still thought of animals as money. Other metals were used, too. The metals could come in any shape. Gold dust was money. Gold bars were money.

4   Today, different countries have different names for money. Sometimes, we call several cents *pennies.* The English call them *pence.* Spanish people call them *centavos* (sen täv′ ōs).

1. Long ago, people used as money
   a. paper.   c. animals.
   b. metal.   d. silver.

2. The word in the story that means *something hard to pick up or carry* is _____.

3. The story says, "In some places, people shaped the gold to look like animals. *They* still thought of animals as money." The word *they* means _____.

4. Which of the following does this story lead you to believe?
   a. People need money to buy things they want.
   b. Gold is good as money when it is very heavy.
   c. Stones are better than feathers as money.

5. What did the special shapes of the metals mean? (Which sentence is exactly like the one in your book?)
   a. Each special shape would be worth something different.
   b. The people would make metals in special shapes.
   c. Some of the special shapes looked like different animals.

6. The main idea of the whole story is that
   a. animals are too heavy to be used as money.
   b. people make animals out of stone.
   c. people have used different kinds of money.

7. The opposite of *take* (in sentence three) is _____.

I'm a Lucky Dog

1   My name is Molly, and I'm a guide dog. I got this job because I'm strong, gentle, and smart.

2   When I was seven weeks old, I went to Guide Dog School. My teacher took me to the store, to church, and to a Girl Scout meeting. Every place I went I learned how to behave. I learned to stay and sit and walk on a leash. Then I learned how to cross streets safely.

3   Soon I met Linda, a young blind woman. We practiced going to the mall, to the store, and to the park. The hardest part was going out to eat. I had to lie under the table and smell all that good food.

4   Now I live with Linda and help her walk to work every day. She takes good care of me. She says I changed her life.

1. Molly is a

    a. boy.   b. blind woman.   c. guide dog.   d. Girl Scout.

2. The word in the story that means *cannot see* is _____.

3. The story says, "My name is Molly, and I'm a guide dog. *I* got this job because I'm strong, gentle, and smart." The word *I* means _____.

4. Which of the following does the story lead you to believe?

    a. Blind people cannot work.

    b. Blind people need help crossing the street.

    c. Blind people do not like dogs.

5. What did Molly learn? (Which sentence is exactly like the one in your book?)

    a. I learned to sit up and beg.

    b. I learned to catch a ball.

    c. I learned to stay and sit and walk on a leash.

6. The main idea of the whole story is that

    a. Guide dogs like to eat out.

    b. Guide dogs like to go to the park.

    c. Guide dogs can help blind people.

7. The opposite of *weak* (paragraph one, sentence two) is _____.

Stop for Fair Rules

1   Once there were no rules to protect workers. Men, women, and even children had to work many hours each day. They were not paid much. Sometimes they got sick. They had to keep working.

2   Then men and women came together to make fair rules for workers. They made good rules. If some workers thought a job was too hard, all the workers could stop working.

3   Sometimes workers stop working when they want more pay. When workers all stop a job together, it is called a "strike."

4   Many years ago, in some Indian tribes, women made the moccasins for the men to wear to war. Sometimes the women leaders in the tribe did not want a war. Then they would stop making moccasins for the men to wear. Were these Indian women going on strike?

1. Once men, women, and children
   a. got no pay.
   c. made bad rules.
   b. were not paid much.
   d. made moccasins.

2. The word in the story that means *to stop work all together* is _____ .

3. The story says, "Men, women, and even children had to work many hours each day. *They* were not paid much." The word *they* means _____ .

4. Which of the following does this story lead you to believe?
   a. All workers need moccasins.
   b. Indians liked to strike.
   c. Once workers did not have fair rules.

5. Why did the Indian women stop making moccasins? (Which sentence is exactly like the one in your book?)
   a. They wanted to go to war, too.
   b. They needed more pay for their families.
   c. Sometimes the women leaders in the tribe did not want a war.

6. The main idea of the whole story is that
   a. all rules are fair.
   b. working makes you sick.
   c. people can make fair rules for themselves.

7. The opposite of *well* (in paragraph one) is _____ .

Old Job or New Job?

1   Some jobs are new. Some jobs are gone. Other jobs are old. We just have new ways of doing them.

2   Long ago, people knew how to make paper by hand. It took a long time for paper to be made this way. After a while, machines were used to make paper. Now people who make paper by hand are not needed any more.

3   Once many people made their own cloth. They got fibers from plants, like flax. They wove the fibers into cloth. They also used plants to make their own dyes for the cloth. Today men and women go to shops to buy many kinds of cloth made by machines.

4   Once people put shoes on horses. Now they put tires on cars.

5   Today, only a few people know how to fly spaceships. Just a few years ago, there were no spaceships. Someday, this may be an old job, too.

1. Once people put shoes on
        a. cars.   c. their feet.
        b. horses.   d. soldiers.

2. The word in the story that means *something that changes the color of cloth* is _____.

3. The story says, "Once people put shoes on horses. Now *they* put tires on cars." The word *they* means _____.

4. Which of the following does this story lead you to believe?
        a. Paper made by hand is the best paper.
        b. Jobs change as people learn new ways of working.
        c. You have to be old to fly a spaceship.

5. How was paper made long ago? (Which sentence is exactly like the one in your book?)
        a. Long ago, paper was made by hand.
        b. Long ago, people knew how to make paper by hand.
        c. Long ago, some people made paper by machine.

6. The main idea of the whole story is that
        a. there are old jobs and new jobs.
        b. old dye is the best.
        c. we don't need spaceships any more.

7. The opposite of *off* (paragraph four, sentence one) is _____.

The Dog Who Could Not Understand

Once a tiger was in a cage. Soon a good woman went by. As soon as the tiger saw the woman, the tiger began to cry. "Please! Please!" it called. "Please, let me out."

"No," said the good woman. "If I do, you will eat me."

"I will not eat you," the tiger said. "Please let me out."

The good woman believed the tiger. She opened the door of the cage. The tiger jumped out. "How stupid you are," the tiger laughed. "Now I am going to eat you."

"Wait!" the woman cried. "It is wrong to eat me. Let us ask others what they think."

"You may ask three others," the tiger said.

The good woman asked a tree. It said, "I give shade. And yet I am cut down. Let the tiger eat you."

Next, the good woman asked a bird. The bird said, "I hurt no one. Yet people hunt and kill me. Let the tiger eat you."

The last one the good woman asked was the road. The road said, "I don't care if the tiger eats you. People could not get along too well without me. Yet all day long people step on me without even a thank you."

The tiger was ready to eat the good woman. Just then a dog came by. "What is going on?" asked the dog. The woman told the dog the whole story.

"I don't understand," said the dog. "The tiger wants to eat you because you put it in a cage?"

"No, no," said the woman. "Some other people put it in a cage."

"Oh," the dog said. "The tiger is going to eat you because you do not have a cage."

"Stupid dog!" the tiger cried. "Don't you understand? I was in the cage. This woman let me out."

"Oh. I see," the dog said. "When the woman was in the cage, you let her out."

"I was in the cage!" the tiger cried. "Like this!" With that, it jumped back into the cage.

At once, the dog shut the door of the cage. "Oh," the dog laughed. "At last I understand!"

The good woman and the dog walked off. The tiger looked after them.

Then he stretched out in the cage. If he waited long enough, another good person would come by.

Now Reader, try to tell this story to a friend.

The Moving Hill

1   Have you ever seen a hill move? Dunes are sand hills that move. As the wind blows, it moves the sand. It moves the sand against something, like a plant or a rock. The wind moves the sand over and over again. Soon a hill begins to grow. The wind blows more sand to the other side of the hill.

2   Sleeping Bear Dune is a big sand dune near one of the Great Lakes. Many people go to see it. It is hard to walk in the sand. So people ride in special cars. These cars have wide, fat tires. They do not need roads.

3   Sand dunes are found near lakes and oceans. They are also found in the desert. We know hills stay in one place. It may take hundreds of years for the weather to shape hills. Most sand dunes are always moving. The wind makes these moving hills fast.

1. Sand hills are moved by
    - a. rocks.
    - b. cars.
    - c. wind.
    - d. lakes.

2. The word in the story that means *sand hills that move* is

    _____ .

3. The story says, "As the wind blows, *it* moves the sand." The word

    it means the _____ .

4. Which of the following does this story lead you to believe?
    - a. The wind blows sand in the ocean.
    - b. The wind helps change the land.
    - c. Many people live on sand dunes.

5. What is hard to do? (Which sentence is exactly like the one in
    your book?)
    - a. It is hard to walk in the sand.
    - b. It is hard to move a hill.
    - c. It is hard to ride in special cars.

6. The main idea of the whole story is that
    - a. cars have flat tires.
    - b. sand dunes are always moving.
    - c. bears like the Great Lakes.

7. The opposite of *thin* (paragraph two, sentence five) is _____ .

The Land of the Reindeer

1   The land of the reindeer is called Lapland. It is a very cold place. Winter is long and summer is short. There is a lot of snow. Reindeer can live there because they have thick fur. With their big feet they can walk on the snow and they can travel long distances. In winter the reindeer go to places that are not so cold to look for good things to eat. In summer it is easier for them to find food.

2   People live in that cold place, too. Sometimes they are called Lapps, but they call themselves the Sabme. Long ago the Sabme followed the reindeer. They lived in tents and camps. Their tents were made of reindeer skin. They made warm clothes from the reindeers' thick fur.

3   Today some of the Sabme still live this way. They move from place to place as they follow the reindeer herds. But more and more Sabme stay in one place and live in houses. Some of them fish, some are farmers, and some work in the towns. The lives of the Sabme are slowly changing.

1. The Sabme followed

     a. horses.   b. fish.   c. reindeer.   d. pigs.

2. The word in the story that means *the things we wear* is

     _____.

3. The story says, "Long ago the Sabme followed the reindeer. *They* lived in tents and camps." The word *they* means _____.

4. Which of the following does the story lead you to believe?

     a. Some Sabme still follow the reindeer.

     b. The Sabme houses are all the same.

     c. The Sabme like to eat fish.

5. Why can reindeer live in a cold place? (Which sentence is exactly like the one in your book?)

     a. Reindeer can live there because they have big teeth.

     b. Reindeer can live there because they like snow.

     c. Reindeer can live there because they have thick fur.

6. The main idea of the whole story is that

     a. today the Sabme live and work in different ways.

     b. reindeer are happy in a cold place.

     c. all the Sabme live in tents and camps.

7. The opposite of *hot* (paragraph one, sentence two) is

     _____.

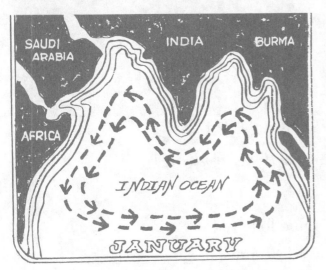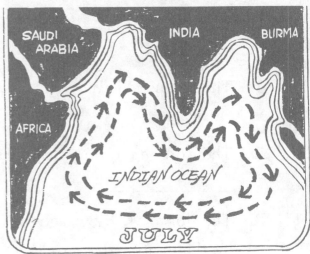

The River in the Ocean

1   The water races. It moves like a fast river. It is called a current. A current is water moving one way. Far from our country, there is a current that moves like a river. This river races faster than any other current in the world. It is in the Indian Ocean.

2   This current is pushed by strong winds. These winds are called monsoon (mon sün′) winds. All summer, the monsoon winds push the current north. The monsoon winds bring heavy rains to many countries.

3   In fall, something happens. The river in the ocean does not race any more. It becomes a slow moving current. After a while, the current stops. But now the monsoon winds begin to blow again. They blow the other way! Now they push the current south.

4   No other river races, slows down, stops, and then goes back the other way.

1. The current moves like a fast
   a. ocean.   c. river.
   b. wind.   d. Indian.

2. The word in the story that means *water moving one way* is

   _____ .

3. The story says, "The water races. *It* moves like a fast river."

   The word *it* means _____ .

4. Which of the following does this story lead you to believe?
   a. All currents are the same.
   b. Winds help make currents.
   c. Indians like the ocean.

5. What do the monsoon winds bring? (Which sentence is exactly like the one in your book?)
   a. The monsoon winds bring Indians to the ocean.
   b. The monsoon winds bring heavy snows to many countries.
   c. The monsoon winds bring heavy rains to many countries.

6. The main idea of the whole story is that
   a. the monsoon winds always blow the same way.
   b. the Indian Ocean has a different kind of current.
   c. winds in summer are stronger than winds in winter.

7. The opposite of *goes* (last sentence) is _____ .

Hurakan,
God of the Big Wind

1   Far out at sea, the wind is blowing. It blows the water into waves. The waves move toward the land. Wave after wave rolls up on the sand. Each wave brings in some sand. It washes up seashells and pieces of wood. Then the water runs back into the sea. It takes sand back with it. When the wind blows hard, the waves are high. They roll up farther on the shore.

2   Every wave changes the shore. The shoreline looks a little different each day. But it is hard to see the change.

3   Very strong winds are called hurricanes. Hurricanes blow down trees and houses. Big waves beat against the shore. In a few hours, the shoreline looks different. It is easy to see the change.

4   Hurricanes are named after Hurakan (hü rə kän′), the West Indian god of the big wind. The hurricane has a good name. It means "to blow away."

FIND THE ANSWERS

1. The wind blows the water into
   - a. pieces of wood.
   - b. hills.
   - c. rain.
   - d. waves.

2. The word in the story that means *some very strong winds* is

   _____ .

3. The story says, "Far out at sea, the wind is blowing. *It* blows the

   water into waves." The word *it* means the _____ .

4. Which of the following does this story lead you to believe?
   - a. Hurricanes are good.
   - b. Hurricanes can hurt people.
   - c. Hurricanes are named after waves.

5. What do waves do to the shore? (Which sentence is exactly like the one in your book?)
   - a. Every wave blows down a tree.
   - b. Every wave changes the shore.
   - c. Every wave has a name.

6. The main idea of the whole story is that
   - a. hurricanes make fast changes in the land.
   - b. waves bring seashells in to shore.
   - c. the West Indians like the wild hurricanes.

7. The opposite of *easy* (paragraph two, sentence three) is

   _____ .

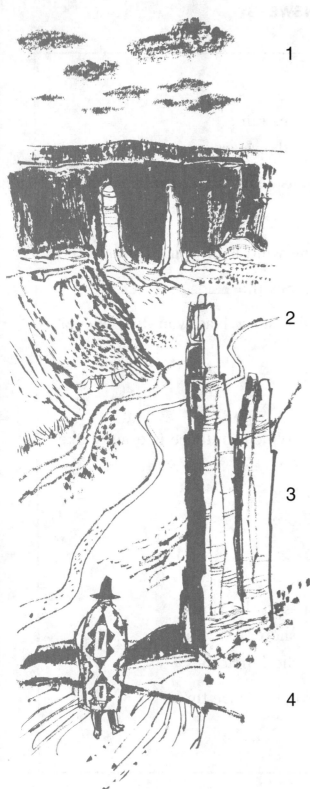

Shapes from the Past

1   The Native Americans looked down at the rock. The rocks had different colors. They had many different shapes. The Native Americans gave the rocks a name. They called them "red rocks standing like people." The rocks had not always looked like standing people. Over a long time, the weather had given the rocks their strange shapes.

2   Weather wears away all rocks. Wind and water turn some rocks into sand and dust. The sand and dust blow away. They become part of the earth. Other rocks, like the red rocks, are changing into strange shapes as they wear away.

3   Wind and rain wear down the soft rocks first. Hard rocks last a long time. In the desert, wind and sand shape the rocks. Some hard rocks look like bridges. Some look like castles. Some rocks look like chimneys without houses. They are called chimney rocks.

4   Someday, all these rocks will have other shapes.

1. The rocks were changed by

    a. the weather.   c. the trees.

    b. the Native Americans.   d. strange people.

2. The word in the story that means *the form of things* is

    _____.

3. The story says, "The rocks had different colors. *They* had many different shapes." The word *they* means _____.

4. Which of the following does the story lead you to believe?

    a. Soft rocks make good bridges.

    b. The land will look different someday.

    c. There is a lot of wind and rain in the desert.

5. What does weather do to rocks? (Which sentence is exactly like the one in your book?)

    a. Weather turns sand into red rocks.

    b. Weather wears away all rocks.

    c. Weather makes Native Americans give rocks names.

6. The main idea of the whole story is that

    a. Native Americans named rocks.

    b. rocks become chimneys.

    c. weather changes rocks.

7. The opposite of *all* (paragraph two, sentence one) is

    _____.

Helmets Old and New

1   Your head is very important. You see, hear, smell, taste, and think with your head. It is easy to hurt your head. You can protect it by wearing a helmet.

2   Helmets have been used for a long time. The first helmets were used by men in battle. The helmets protected their heads from being hit and from the sharp points of spears. The old helmets were made of metal and were very heavy.

3   Today many people wear helmets. Construction workers wear them in case something falls on their head. Police officers and firefighters wear helmets for protection. Baseball players wear helmets in case they get hit by the ball. Football players wear helmets, too. The new helmets are made of plastic. They come in all colors and sizes. They are light and easy to wear.

4   There are even helmets for kids. If you fall off your bike, you can bump your head. A helmet will protect you. Wearing a helmet is a good idea.

1. The first helmets were used by
   a. cave men.   c. workers.
   b. men in battle   d. football players.

2. The word in the story that means *keep from getting hurt* is
   _____.

3. The story says, "It is easy to hurt your head. You can protect *it* by wearing a helmet." The word *it* means _____.

4. Which of the following does the story lead you to believe?
   a. The old helmets didn't work.
   b. A helmet can save your life.
   c. Only men wear helmets.

5. What are the new helmets made of? (Which sentence is exactly like the one in your book?)
   a. The new helmets are made of metal.
   b. The new helmets are made of steel.
   c. The new helmets are made of plastic.

6. The main idea of the whole story is that
   a. helmets have changed.
   b. grownups should wear helmets.
   c. people don't like to wear helmets.

7. The opposite of *short* (paragraph two, sentence one) is
   _____.

Ghost Town

1   The wind blows down the empty street. There are no cars or people on the street. Grass and weeds grow there. The wind blows through houses. The boards shake. No one cares. The houses are gray and empty. This is a ghost town.

2   Most ghost towns are in the mountains. They were built near old mines. Men came to work in the mines. They were looking for gold and silver.

3   Men and women came with their families. They built houses. Soon there were stores selling food and other things. There were many shops. The town was a busy place.

4   In twenty years, the gold and silver were gone. The families left. The people who owned the shops left. All the people moved on. Today, only empty, old buildings are there. Can you tell why it is called a ghost town?

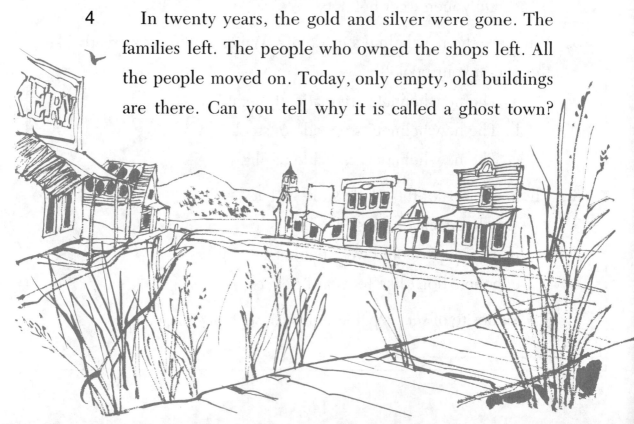

1. When the gold and silver were gone, the people
   - a. cried.
   - c. sang.
   - b. left.
   - d. stayed.

2. The words in the story that mean *a place no one lives in any more* are _____ .

3. The story says, "Men and women came with their families. *They* built houses." The word *they* means _____ .

4. Which of the following does this story lead you to believe?
   - a. Many families live in ghost towns.
   - b. People make a town live and grow.
   - c. Most towns are gray and empty.

5. Where are most of the ghost towns? (Which sentence is exactly like the one in your book?)
   - a. Most ghost towns are in South America.
   - b. Most ghost towns are in the mountains.
   - c. Most ghost towns are busy places.

6. The main idea of the whole story is that
   - a. some towns that were once busy became ghost towns.
   - b. houses and stores are built in mines.
   - c. gold is very difficult to find in a busy old town.

7. The opposite of *came* (in paragraph four, sentence two) is

   _____ .

The Pike Across the Road

1   The roads of England were bad. It was hard to go from town to town. In the spring, the mud was deep. Horses fell into holes. Wheels got stuck in the mud. People could not walk on the roads. They had to walk through fields and woods. The soldiers could not march.

2   In 1751, England began to build new roads. The new roads could be used all year long. People and goods could move from town to town.

3   People had to pay to use the new roads. Gates were put up. A long pole called a pike was placed across the road. People gave money to the gatekeeper. Then the gatekeeper turned the pike out of the way. The roads were called turnpikes.

4   The word *turnpike* is still used today. Our wide turnpikes go all across the land. They make it easy for people to go from place to place.

1. The mud was deep on the roads in the
   a. summer.   c. winter.
   f. fall.   d. spring.

2. The word in the story that means *a long pole placed across a road* is _____ .

3. The story says, "People could not walk on the roads. *They* had to walk through fields and woods." The word *they* means

   _____ .

4. Which of the following does this story lead you to believe?
   a. No one liked the new roads.
   b. People like to pay money to the gatekeeper.
   c. Traveling on turnpikes is faster than on old roads.

5. What did the people do when they couldn't walk on the roads? (Which sentence is exactly like the one in your book?)
   a. They had to walk through fields and woods.
   b. They had to walk through the towns.
   c. They had to march with the soldiers.

6. The main idea of the whole story is that
   a. England is full of mud.
   b. people need good roads.
   c. soldiers can't march.

7. The opposite of *good* (in sentence one) is _____ .

The Peach Basket Game

1   Basketball is an American game. A man named James Naismith made it up in 1891. He wanted a game to play inside in the winter. The first real game was played in 1892.

2   Naismith put up two peach baskets. There were nine players on each side. The players tried to throw the ball into the baskets. There were no holes in the bottom of the baskets. When a ball went into the basket, it stayed there. The game had to stop. A player climbed up to get the ball. It was a slow game. After a while, net baskets were used. The bottoms were cut out of the baskets.

3   At first, many persons could play. Now only ten team members play the game. There are five players on each side. Basketball today is a very fast game.

4   Once basketball was played only in this country. Now basketball is played in many lands.

1. James Naismith wanted a game to play in the
   - a. spring.
   - c. fall.
   - b. winter.
   - d. summer.

2. The word in the story that means *something you play for fun* is _____.

3. The story says, "When a ball went into the basket, *it* stayed there." The word *it* means _____.

4. Which of the following does this story lead you to believe?
   - a. We still use peach baskets when we play this game.
   - b. A good game does not always have to be a new game.
   - c. Basketball began as a farmer's game.

5. What happened when the ball went into the peach basket? (Which sentence is exactly like the one in your book?)
   - a. When a ball went in the basket, they called Mr. Naismith.
   - b. When a ball went in the basket, the bottoms were cut out.
   - c. When a ball went in the basket, it stayed there.

6. The main idea of the whole story is that
   - a. peaches are good to eat.
   - b. most games are not much fun.
   - c. basketball is a good game.

7. The opposite of *tops* (paragraph two, sentence four) is _____.

Save the Whales

1   Whales are big animals that live in the ocean. They are not fish. They have warm bodies and breathe air. The blue whale is the biggest animal in the world. Whales can live in very cold water because under their skin they have a thick layer of fat to keep them warm. The fat is called blubber.

2   For hundreds of years people have hunted whales. The oil from their blubber was used for lamps. It was also made into soap, paint, candles, and shoe polish. The meat was used for food. All parts of the whale were used. Most of the whales were killed.

3   Then, some people wanted the killing to stop. They showed why whales are important. Many Americans stopped buying things made from whales. In 1971 a 14-year-old girl started a group called Save the Whales.

4   All these people worked to change the laws about hunting whales. Some countries still hunt these animals. But more and more people are understanding that it is important to protect whales, not kill them.

1. People hunted whales for their

     a. fur.   b. horns.   c. oil.   d. tails.

2. The word in the story that means *fat* is _____.

3. The story says, "Whales are big animals that live in the ocean. *They* are not fish." The word *they* means _____.

4. Which of the following does the story lead you to believe?

     a. All the whales were killed.

     b. Many people like whales.

     c. Whales don't like cold water.

5. Where do whales live? (Which sentence is exactly like the one in your book?)

     a. Whales live in America.

     b. Whales live in lakes and rivers.

     c. Whales are big animals that live in the ocean.

6. The main idea of the whole story is that

     a. people learned that whales should be protected.

     b. whales are getting bigger.

     c. whales get along well with people.

7. The opposite of *selling* (paragraph three, sentence three) is _____.

The Big Dogs

1   The Sioux Indians lived near the plains. They hunted buffalo. But they did not go far. They had no horses. They lived this way for many years.

2   There were no horses in this country until 1519. Then soldiers and explorers came from Spain. They brought horses with them. Some of the horses were lost. They became wild.

3   About 1600, the Sioux Indians found some of the wild horses. They thought the horses were big dogs. The Indians soon learned how wonderful the "big dogs" were. On horses, the Sioux could follow the buffalo for many miles. Now the Sioux did not have to stay in one place.

4   Soon the Sioux became a strong people. They took what they wanted from other Indians. The other Indians could not catch them. But before long, other Indians had horses, too.

5   Once Indians had horses, their lives changed quickly in many ways.

1. Horses were brought from
   - a. the plains.
   - c. Spain.
   - b. Mexico.
   - d. the hills.

2. The word in the story that means *big open fields* or *flat country* is

   _____ .

3. The story says, "Some of the horses were lost. *They* became wild."

   The word *they* means _____ .

4. Which of the following does this story lead you to believe?
   - a. The wild horse has always lived in North America.
   - b. Horses made an Indian nation strong.
   - c. Indians hunted horses for food.

5. What did the Sioux do when they became strong? (Which sentence is exactly like the one in your book?)
   - a. They took what they wanted from other Indians.
   - b. They took all the Indians they wanted.
   - c. They turned their big dogs into horses to ride.

6. The main idea of the whole story is that
   - a. explorers and soldiers are wild men from Spain.
   - b. the horse changed the lives of the Indians.
   - c. strong people who have horses become Indians.

7. The opposite of *go* (paragraph three, sentence five) is _____ .

Books in Chains

1   Have you ever seen a book in chains? Long ago, very few people could read. They did not have books at home. Books were kept in special libraries. Sometimes the books were chained to tables.

2   In those days, people had to write all books by hand. They painted beautiful pictures in many of the books. Only one book could be made at a time. Making a book was very slow work. Sometimes it took years just to make one book.

3   Later, printing machines were made. Machines could print many books at one time. Soon people began to learn to read. They wanted more books. Better printing machines were made to give the people more books. Now printing machines run day and night. They print thousands of books in just a few days.

4   How many different books do you use in school today?

FIND THE ANSWERS

1. Long ago, very few people could
    - a. read.
    - b. dance.
    - c. laugh.
    - d. jump.

2. The word in the story that means *something not like other things* is _____ .

3. The story says, "Soon people began to learn to read. *They* wanted more books." The word *they* means _____ .

4. Which of the following does this story lead you to believe?
    - a. Books are important to people.
    - b. Books must have chains.
    - c. It is not good to put pictures in books.

5. What happened when people began to learn to read? (Which sentence is exactly like the one in your book?)
    - a. They wanted more printing machines.
    - b. They wanted more books.
    - c. They wanted more teachers.

6. The main idea of the whole story is that
    - a. machines cannot print books with many pictures in them.
    - b. making books with printing machines takes a long time.
    - c. printing machines made it easy for people to get books.

7. The opposite of *night* (paragraph three, sentence six) is

    _____ .

Sixteen Left Feet

1   We measure things in feet. We measure things in yards. We also measure things in rods. One rod is the same as $5\frac{1}{2}$ yards. It is the same as $16\frac{1}{2}$ feet.

2   Once the rod was called a "rood." Land was measured in roods. People did not know just how long a rood was. How do you think they found out?

3   One way was to stop sixteen people as they came out of church. The people could be tall. The people could be short. But there had to be sixteen in all. Each one had to put the left foot out. Each left foot had to be behind another left foot. Sixteen left feet made one rood.

4   Now you know how we got the word "rod." Can you find out how we got the words "feet" and "yard"?

one rod

158

1. Sixteen people were stopped as they came out of
   a. the store.
   c. the sky.
   b. the ground.
   d. the church.

2. The word in the story that means *a building where people go to pray* is _____ .

3. The story says, "One rod is the same as 5½ yards. *It* is the same as 16½ feet." The word *it* means _____ .

4. Which of the following does this story lead you to believe?
   a. Measuring sixteen left feet was a poor way to measure.
   b. Only sixteen people went to church on the same day.
   c. Only the feet of tall people could be measured easily.

5. What did the people do? (Which sentence is exactly like the one in your book?)
   a. Each one tried to grow very tall.
   b. Each one had to put the left foot out.
   c. Each one took off the left shoe at church.

6. The main idea of the whole story is that
   a. only left feet were used in measuring roods.
   b. people once used rods and roods to measure things.
   c. short people are better than tall people for measuring.

7. The opposite of *short* (paragraph three, sentence two) is

   _____ .

Make a Fist

1   "Make a fist," Mary Brown said. The boy made a fist. Mary Brown took the heel and toe of the sock. She tried to make them meet around the fist. If the heel and toe met around the fist, the sock would fit the boy. This was how she measured size.

2   Bob Smith needed three yards of cloth. He put one part of the cloth against his nose. He held the rest of the cloth out as far as his arm could go. "One yard," Bob Smith said. He did this three times. He now had three yards of cloth. This was how he measured cloth. Your grandparents may have measured things this way.

3   Today, we do not have to make a fist to get the right size for socks. We do not have to put cloth against our noses to measure it. How do we measure? Do we guess, or do we know?

1. The boy made a fist to
   a. start a fight with someone.   c. stand on his head.
   b. see if the sock would fit.   d. eat a sock.

2. The word in the story that means *a hand closed up tight* is

   _____ .

3. The story says, "Bob Smith needed three yards of cloth. *He* put one part of the cloth against his nose." The word *he* means

   _____ .

4. Which of the following does this story lead you to believe?
   a. We have better ways to measure cloth today.
   b. Bob Smith had a big nose and long arms.
   c. Bob Smith needed to measure many yards of cloth.

5. What did Mary Brown try to do? (Which sentence is exactly like the one in your book?)
   a. She tried to start a fight with the boy.
   b. She tried to measure the cloth with her nose.
   c. She tried to make them meet around the fist.

6. The main idea of the whole story is that
   a. Bob Smith was a very clever man who invented measures.
   b. cloth cannot be measured by using your arms.
   c. people used their fists and arms to measure things.

7. The opposite of *toe* (in sentence three) is _____ .

Something for Nothing

1   Once there was no zero. To write numerals for sixty-three, people wrote 63. To write six hundred three, people wrote 6 3. The space was there to mean "not any" tens. Sometimes people did not remember the space. It was hard to see and to read.

2   Later, people used a dot to hold the space. Six hundred three looked like this 6.3. But the dot was hard to see. So people put a circle around it like this 6⊙3. Then people could see the dot. They remembered the space.

3   At last, only the circle around the dot was used. It was like a zero. This is one story of how the zero came to be used.

4   Now zero has many important uses. Zero tells how many. Can you tell some other ways zero is used?

162

1. Sometimes people did not remember
        a. to read.   c. a story.
        b. to eat.   d. a space.

2. The word in the story that means *a circle that means "not any"*

    is _____ .

3. The story says, "Then the people could see the dot. *They* remembered the space." The word *they* means _____ .

4. Which of the following does this story lead you to believe?
        a. People long ago didn't know how to make dots.
        b. We cannot count without the zero.
        c. People like to tell stories about the zero.

5. What was the space there for? (Which sentence is exactly like the one in your book?)
        a. The space was there to make room for people.
        b. The space was there to mean "not any" tens.
        c. The space was there to make reading hard.

6. The main idea of the whole story is that
        a. the zero is important.
        b. dots look pretty in circles.
        c. you must never use a zero.

7. The opposite of *forget* (in sentence five) is _____ .

Earthquake!

1   Sometimes the land shakes and sometimes it moves. Sometimes the land cracks. This is called an earthquake. No one knows where or when an earthquake will happen. No one knows how big it will be. But if it happens in a city, things change fast.

2   In 1989 there was a big earthquake in San Francisco. It happened in the afternoon when people were going home from work. Bridges and buildings fell down. Streets cracked. Water pipes broke. Fires burned. Many people were hurt, and some people were killed.

3   Soon helpers came. People who were hurt went to hospitals. Firefighters put out the fires. Workers fixed the pipes. New streets and bridges were built. People moved to new homes.

4   The earthquake lasted fifteen seconds. It took many years to fix what the earthquake did in fifteen seconds.

1. In 1989 there was a big earthquake in
   a. New York.   c. San Francisco.
   b. a little town.   d. a pipe.

2. The word in the story that means *places that help people who are hurt* is _____.

3. The story says, "No one knows where or when an earthquake will happen. No one knows how big *it* will be." The word *it* means _____.

4. Which of the following does this story lead you to believe?
   a. All earthquakes are big.
   b. People like earthquakes.
   c. An earthquake can happen at any time.

5. What time of day did the earthquake happen? (Which sentence is exactly like the one in your book?)
   a. It happened early in the morning.
   b. It happened in the afternoon when people were going home from work.
   c. It happened at night when people were sleeping.

6. The main idea of the whole story is that
   a. an earthquake can change things fast.
   b. earthquakes are fun.
   c. earthquakes last a long time.

7. The opposite of *little* (paragraph one, sentence five) is _____.

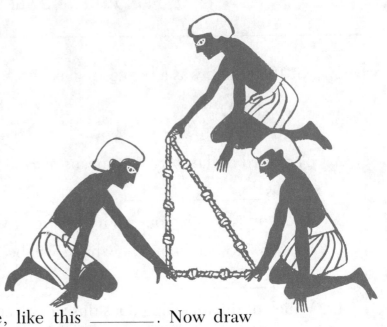

The Rope Stretchers

1   Draw a straight line, like this _____. Now draw another line, like this └_____. Do you know what we call this? A right angle.

2   Long ago, in Egypt, right angles were used to measure land. People who did this work were called "rope stretchers." They used long, heavy ropes. Each rope had 12 knots. The space between the knots was always the same.

3   It took three people to make a right angle. One person held both ends of the rope. The second person counted 3 knots from one end of the rope. The next person counted 4 knots from the other end of the rope. Then they pulled the rope tight. The "rope stretchers" had made a right angle.

4   We still measure land. But our way of measuring is different. We do not use ropes. We use special tools. Have you ever seen people using these special tools?

FIND THE ANSWERS

1. Long ago, in Egypt, right angles were used to
   a. measure land.   c. give three people jobs.
   b. stretch rope.   d. make ropes heavy.

2. The word in the story that means *ropes or strings tied together*

   is _____ .

3. The story says, "People who did this work were called "rope stretchers." *They* used long, heavy ropes." The word *they*

   means _____ .

4. Which of the following does this story lead you to believe?
   a. People never used right angles to measure land in Egypt.
   b. No one can draw a really straight line.
   c. It was not easy work to measure the land.

5. How many people did it take to make a right angle? (Which sentence is exactly like the one in your book?)
   a. It took four people to make a right angle.
   b. It took three people to make a right angle.
   c. It took twelve people to make a right angle.

6. The main idea of the whole story is that
   a. people in Egypt had a lot of ropes.
   b. people in Egypt carried ropes on stretchers.
   c. rope stretchers measured the land in Egypt.

7. The opposite of *loose* (paragraph three, sentence five) is

   _____ .

A Dusty Way to Count

1   Have you ever seen an abacus (ab′ ə kəs)? An abacus has rows of beads on wires. The beads are called counters. The counters can be moved up and down on the wires. People in ancient times used the abacus. Some people in Asia still use it. But in most places new ways of counting are used.

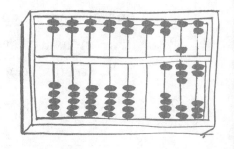

2   In ancient times, an abacus was made in the dust or sand. People would draw lines in the dust for ones, for tens, for hundreds, for thousands. Stones were put on the lines. The stones were used as counters.

3   Later, sticks were used as lines. Stones with holes were put on the sticks.

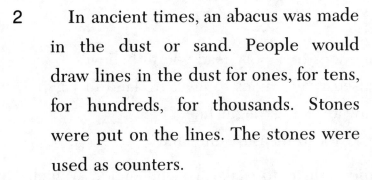

4   Some people used the tops of tables as an abacus. They would draw lines on the table. They used pebbles as counters. Our word "counter" comes from this way of counting.

1. On an abacus, the counters are
   a. bones.   c. sticks.
   b. beads.   d. wires.

2. The word in the story that means *small stones* is _____ .

3. The story says, "People in ancient times used the abacus. Some people in Asia still use *it*." The word *it* means _____ .

4. Which of the following does this story lead you to believe?
   a. Ancient people liked beads and stones with holes.
   b. People in Asia did not need to count things.
   c. It was not easy to use an abacus made in dust.

5. What was put on the lines in the dust? (Which sentence is exactly like the one in your book?)
   a. Beads were put on the lines.
   b. Sticks were put on the lines.
   c. Stones were put on the lines.

6. The main idea of the whole story is that
   a. beads look good on wires or on sticks.
   b. the best way to count is with beads or stones.
   c. ancient people used the abacus for counting.

7. The opposite of *goes* (paragraph four, sentence four) is

   _____ .

Fill in your record chart after each test. Beside the page numbers, put a one for each correct question. Put zero in the box of each question you missed. At the far right, put your total. Seven is a perfect score for each test.

When you finish all the tests in a concept, total your scores by question. Thirty-six is the highest possible score for each question.

When you have taken several tests, check to see which questions you get right each time. Which ones are you missing? Find the places where you need help. For example, if you are missing Question 3 often, ask for help in learning to use directing words.

As you begin each concept, copy the chart onto lined paper. Down the left side are the test page numbers. Across the top are the question numbers and the kinds of questions. For example, each Question 1 in this book asks you to recall a fact. Your scores for each question show how well you are learning each skill.

Your Reading Scores

Concept I

	Question 1 fact	Question 2 vocabulary	Question 3 antecedent	Question 4 inference	Question 5 confirming content	Question 6 main idea	Question 7 vocabulary-opposites	Total for Page
Page 15								
17								
19								
21								
23								
25								
27								
29								
31								
33								
35								
37								
39								
41								
43								
45								
47								
49								
55								
57								
59								
61								
63								
65								
67								
69								
71								
73								
75								
77								
79								
81								
83								
85								
87								
89								
Totals by question								

Your Reading Scores
Concept II

	Question 1 fact	Question 2 vocabulary	Question 3 antecedent	Question 4 inference	Question 5 confirming content	Question 6 main idea	Question 7 vocabulary-opposites	Total for Page
Page 95								
97								
99								
101								
103								
105								
107								
109								
111								
113								
115								
117								
119								
121								
123								
125								
127								
129								
135								
137								
139								
141								
143								
145								
147								
149								
151								
153								
155								
157								
159								
161								
163								
165								
167								
169								
Totals by question								